The Girl in a Drawer

by

Dee Larcombe
and Ronald Clements

Published by New Generation Publishing in 2020

Copyright © Dee Larcombe and Ronald Clements 2020

First Edition

British Library Cataloguing in Publication Data

A catalogue record for this book is available from the British Library.

ISBN 978-1-78955-906-4

Cover design: Mark Larcombe

www.newgeneration-publishing.com

New Generation Publishing

'Dee Larcombe has given us a book that is joy to read. From its poignant beginning to its powerful conclusion, it is a testimony to an indomitable spirit that says "no matter what tries to knock me down, I will rise up and win through."

'The final story of reconciliation with her childhood captors is the crowning glory of an autobiography that page after page shows the wisdom of constantly coming to terms with life's challenges through a genuine faith, a positive mindset, a practical approach, a sense of humour, a realistic vulnerability, and above all an absolute honesty.

'*The Girl in a Drawer* is a story of a childhood captivity that captivated me from start to finish.'
Revd. Dr Hugh Osgood
Free Churches Moderator and President of Churches Together in England

'Dee's compelling story encourages and challenges us as we learn how she has overcome dire circumstances. It is heart-breaking to read *The Girl in a Drawer* and how Dee endured a devastating and turbulent young life. However, Dee has experienced profound healing, forgiveness and reconciliation. She has emerged with a dedicated and generous spirit.'
Keiko C. Holmes OBE
Founder of Agape World

'*The Girl in a Drawer* is a beautiful account of an uplifting life story. Dee writes with real warmth and humour – a testament to the freedom she discovers in the midst of so much disruption. I am glad she has "opened the drawer" on such a vivid description of her life.'
Revd. Jon Ward
Rector of St. John's, West Wickham

For

my four delightful grandchildren

Aaron, Matthew, Amy
&
Sofia

Dee Larcombe was born in Hong Kong, where her father was stationed prior to the Second World War. She trained as a nurse in Bristol and, with her husband Geoff, joined Regions Beyond Missionary Union, serving as a missionary in north India. She is now retired and living in Greater London.

Ronald Clements is a full-time writer, researcher and filmmaker, living in Kent. He writes Christian biographies and resource materials, as well as writing and directing documentaries and video promotions.

www.ronaldclements.com

Contents

Prologue

The girl in a drawer. That's me – Dominica Deirdre Danielle Larcombe. Dee for short – which was my husband's idea – and which would have been considerably quicker to write on all those fiddly forms that airlines used to hand out (and still do) as you descend from thirty thousand feet onto the tarmac of a new country. Something that I have had to do on numerous occasions.

Still, I doubt if you picked up this book to read about the fiddly forms I have filled in during my lifetime. But I thought you may be curious to know about my name and how I got it. After all, it took four men to figure it out!

And I thought you might be interested in the drawer. A fairly common old wooden thing, it has to be said. The sort you would have found in the chest of drawers that your great aunt and uncle or your grandparents kept in their bedroom. But mine was in a prison in Hong Kong.

And now an apology because I am not going to start my story there at all. No. Imagine an eight-year-old little girl in pigtails and second-hand clothes, standing on the doorstep of a house at the very edge of a village called Norton, on the outskirts of Stourbridge, just outside Birmingham... feeling all alone.

Chapter 1

Across the Threshold

My first impressions of *Bethany*, number 10 Covert Lane, were that it was a nice house – a semi-detached, with a garage, and bay windows beneath a mock Tudor gable – and that it was particularly quiet, standing as it did halfway along a cul-de-sac and having a cemetery opposite the front door. I guess that Mr and Mrs Pearson, the latest in my line of foster parents, didn't trouble over the tombstones. Mind you, as loyal members of a Protestant chapel, it being a Roman Catholic graveyard may have been a dilemma. This was April 1950 after all.

It was a very different world then. Chronic uncertainty reigned. The king, George VI, was in failing health. Britain was still emerging from beneath the wreckage of the Second World War. The end of food restrictions and ration books was another four years away. The vast majority of the population could only dream of owning a fridge or a car. And one channel TV was still waiting for the coronation of Queen Elizabeth in order to become popular.

But as I stood on the Pearsons' doorstep, in a thin frock and a dark blazar, none of this was worrying me. I had my own difficulties to contend with. My mother was ill – lost in worlds of her own. My father was unwell, trying to keep his job in the army. And I had left my little sister, Jean, with a family of strangers living in a house an eternity away. Now I was somewhere else, wondering who these new people who lived across the threshold were and, more importantly, what they would be like. They were my third set of carers inside eighteen months.

I have to be honest. I felt abandoned. I knew that my father was doing his best to provide for his children, in a situation that was extremely difficult for him. But from my point of view I had been shipped out, into and out of Hong Kong (where I was born) too many times, been berthed in Singapore at least twice, and ferried around a succession of unwelcoming British relatives. I wanted to find a home. Yet here I was, being delivered into the hands of complete strangers.

Of course, I didn't just turn up on the doorstep by myself. My Dad took me to the house, stayed overnight, and then left the next day. He came again five weeks later, arriving late afternoon one Saturday, leaving on the Sunday. In between and afterwards possibly he wrote to me, but I don't remember. One by one I was losing my family. My mother was in hospital in Southampton. Jean was in Birkenhead, Liverpool. And my father was waving goodbye as the door closed behind him. Nevertheless, in the midst of this childhood turmoil, Geoff and Vi Pearsons' home turned out to be a haven for me. Perhaps even, if you like, my salvation in what could have been a very different story.

Geoff Pearson was a kind, careful man, softly spoken, balding with a large forehead. Like most men in the fifties, he always wore a tie and he carried at least two pens in the breast pocket of his tweed jacket. He had a great love of photography and was full of ideas to keep me occupied.

Vi had her own talents – she was a milliner – and there was ample time for me to sit with her, watching her at work on the hats she carefully constructed, and using the offcuts for my own games. Her sharp scissors were also used to dispense with my long black hair. I was very fond of my pigtails. She, on the other hand, thought they were a bother. Needless to say, I was in no position to protest and endured her restyling. In next to no time I had been reduced to the plain bob I wore for a good many years after.

Geoff and Vi had no children of their own and I benefited greatly from their love and care. There were more than enough hugs on offer. Vi – as was the norm – was a stay-at-home mother and always around for me. Geoff taught me how to take photographs and how to develop the

4

first photo he took of me. We had a piece of blueprint paper and laid it out in the sun, washing it in water after the picture had appeared. They gave me an expensive looking handmade black rabbit. As far as I can remember, this was my first proper toy. She was dressed in a very fine floral outfit and shoes, with white knitted ears and paws, and a spread of superior wiry whiskers. Best of all, I got bedtime stories every evening in a bedroom that was all my own.

The Pearsons rapidly became my mum and dad. For over three months I was cosseted and coddled, which was what I craved. Wisely though, Vi never allowed me to call her 'Mummy', much as I wanted to. She remained 'Auntie Vi' throughout my stay. Still, she was very happy to have me clamber onto her lap for cuddles, delivered motherly advice on my behaviour, taught me Bible stories and encouraged me to pray, cared enough to listen to my quandaries, and wiped my tears with the handkerchief she kept in her pocket. Such was our relationship that I invited them to my wedding. I still have an old cassette tape, on which Geoff relates stories of my time with them, that he mailed to me after I sent him a book about my expedition to the source of the Yangtze River – well, nearly to the source, as you will hear...

Added to this care and cosseting was a great opportunity to enjoy being outdoors. I had been raised in Hong Kong, toddling around without shoes, out in the open, untroubled by the weather for hours on end. There had also been slow sea voyages from and to Asia. Seven or eight weeks to play out on deck, as the liners ploughed their way across the Indian Ocean, sailed the Suez Canal, and picked their way through the Straits of Gibraltar to the UK and back again.

The Pearsons had a lovely long lawn at the back of the house, where I could play without supervision. Pedmore Common was a short walk away. At the end of Covert Lane, the road narrowed to a dirt path that ran through a wood, past the old sand pits and rifle range, and on towards the wonderfully named Sugarloaf Farm and Bunker's Hill. Beyond these lay open countryside and lovely wide skies.

Of course, day-to-day life wasn't without its difficulties. There was one time when I was in some pain. The lady next door, a Mrs Johnson, was a retired nursing sister; strict, thin, and an old battle-axe according to Geoff. She had no doubt what the problem was.

'You know what is wrong,' she berated Vi. 'The child hasn't enough clothes.'

She may well have been right. I was resisting Vi's desires for me to wear long stockings and clinging to the notion that I could still dress in Britain as I had done in Hong Kong.

'Give her a good bath and put Sloan's liniment on. She could get rheumatic fever.'

Sloan's – originally manufactured for use on horses – had become something of a cure-all. Whether it cured me, I cannot say. It stung my legs beyond endurance and I was certainly in pain when I was put to bed. Thereafter, Vi organised my wardrobe, not me.

On another occasion, Vi sent me to down to the main road to post a letter, generously giving me a shilling for ice-cream at Brewers, the local shop. When I returned, I had posted the letter and lost the shilling. Still, Vi didn't get annoyed. She said we would pray and that I should go back to the postbox in the wall and wait for the postman to come and empty it; these being the days when children could do such things. The postbox didn't contain the shilling, but when the postman had gone on his way, I spotted the coin in the grass by the wall. I came back very pleased that God had answered my prayer, but I'm not sure I ever got that ice-cream.

School was the biggest bugbear. For a start, I had not had a good beginning to my education. Continually moving around meant I rarely got established in one place before I was expected to settle at another. Long sea voyages had meant makeshift lessons on board ships and in classes in far-flung army schools. At Norton, somewhat belated in mid-May, Vi bought me a new red blazer and a grey skirt and walked me to the school in Stourbridge, where each day I shrank into my seat at the back of the classroom, maintaining as low a profile as I could manage.

I later discovered I am dyslexic. This was a real disability in the 1950s when the problem was not readily recognised and there was little or no help for 'poor' pupils. Sadly, anyone unable to read or write was just considered 'thick'. To this day I still read words back to front and have been known to say words back to front too!

I was also all too aware that I was 'in care'. At a time when 'everyone' had a mum and dad at home, it was apparent to the other children that I must have no father or mother. This was a real stigma for an eight-year-old, back of the classroom, not-good-at-much little girl to grapple with.

Not that I was without friends. I remember being invited to a birthday party a couple of doors down from the Pearsons; the home of a girl called Jane. I was so eager to be seen to have a mother that when the party was over, I insisted on waiting for Vi to collect me. Everyone else's parents duly arrived. Of course, Vi didn't. 'Our' house was no more than twenty yards away. Eventually, long after all the children had left, Jane's Mum sent me home. When Vi questioned my late arrival, I earnestly explained my desire to have her pick me up like all the other mothers had done.

Shortly afterwards, in July, my father did arrive to take me home. The Pearsons were only offering temporary foster care, not adoption. Not that I think my father was considering having Jean and me adopted. My mother came too, but she was not coping well at all. I had found a Bible verse that I thought would help her. However, when I asked her to read it, she looked at it for a moment, and then turned and went out into the hallway without a word. I was so disappointed.

The next day my few clothes were packed up; the precious rabbit left behind. Then I said goodbyes to the couple who had given me a stable home and a fantastic few months of memories. There was no doubt I was going to miss them, but it was many years before I understood there was much more to my short stay than I realised.

In a funny sort of way, in entering Geoff and Vi's house, I crossed a more meaningful threshold. It was as though a door opened to the promise of a future that would not always be blighted by trouble. I could rarely remember a time when our family had not been pitched into one crisis or another. My placement with the Pearsons did not last long, but in the story of my life it was not insignificant.

After the final hugs, I followed my father and mother down the garden path, out onto the lane, and began yet another journey. I don't remember if I cried or whether I stoically accepted this was just what happened in life. I had every reason to weep if I wanted to. Yet any emotion of loss had to be balanced with the knowledge that I was going *home*. We would be a family again. I would see Jean. I would have a mother and father – my real ones.

But... there was a but. When I did get home, what would be waiting for me? And, more importantly, how long would it be before I was sent away again? Not long enough as it turned out.

Chapter 2

Almost Home

I don't want to give you the impression that my mother was not a good Mum to me. That isn't the case. As I will explain later, she cared for me through one of the most testing times of what was in many ways a tragic life. But in the late 1940s, once her mental illness began to develop, things became very difficult. She was only twenty-nine; I was six and Jean was one. Thereafter, my Dad did his best to keep his family together, but when I returned from Norton and Jean arrived back from the house in Birkenhead in summer 1950, the situation was far from satisfactory.

Our home was in the married quarters of the army barracks at Netley, Southampton. My father was Sergeant Alfred Taylor. He had been a private in the Second World War, but then was rapidly promoted to Captain, Acting Sergeant, and Sergeant. He was a gentle man, very caring. I guess this is one of the reasons why, having decided to make a life for himself in the army, he enrolled for the Royal Army Medical Corps (RAMC), where he worked as an orderly.

Dad was average height for the time, well under six foot, probably a bit slimmer than most. The army no doubt kept him fit, but throughout his life he never put much weight on. He had brown hair, brown eyes, and the roundest pair of glasses you would ever find. Once he left the army, he became fond of having a moustache. I have a wonderful photo of him leaning on the railing of a ship's deck, resplendent in a handlebar 'tache.

As a father, he wasn't particularly strict, but (like all 1940s parents) he expected children to be obedient. He played with us a lot when Mum wasn't able to. I have a lovely memory of him carting home an old mattress and laying it out on the living room floor, so that Jean and I could learn to do gymnastics.

If he had a great fault, it was the inability to say 'no' whenever a request came his way. He was not a strong character and was forever wanting to please others. Frequently, he would go short himself, while finding the money for my mother's needs and our care. When our foster parents wanted something, he was always willing to pay. Given a need, I am sure he would have handed over his last penny.

Mum was a very different character. She was not British. Russian, in fact; born out in the remoteness of south Siberia, close to the border with 'Outer' Mongolia. I'm afraid she seemed to have little affection for her homeland. There were no accounts of the curious culture and customs of the country. She didn't entertain me with bedtime tales her mother taught her. She never spoke Russian, not even to teach us a few children's words. (She did, however, speak French and her English was impeccable.) Foodwise, the only thing I remember her making that was not British was yoghurt.

She had a vivid personality and, unlike my Dad (in spite of all the travelling he did), she was adventurous. She wanted to see the world and to some extent that wish was fulfilled. In this way I am very much like her and I have certainly realised her dreams of travel.

As a young woman, Mum was pretty. Looking at her photograph, it is not hard to see why my father fell for her – a beauty from what must have seemed a very enigmatic, unexplored part of the world as far as he was concerned. She had a lovely open expression when she smiled, blessed with very dark brown hair and eyes. Tragically, by the time we were in Netley, her face was disfigured. A facial nerve had been cut during an operation in Hong Kong. When she came round from the anaesthetic, she found that the right side of her face had fallen. It was devastating for her. From then on her appearance was always lopsided; a feature which seemed to exaggerate her plight, as first her growing forgetfulness developed and then her schizophrenia became evident.

Before I was sent to the Pearsons, my mother had been in hospital two or three times. The unit where my father worked – the Royal Victoria Military Hospital – did have a mental health wing. However, I don't know if this facility was men-only. If so, there would have been an added burden on my father, travelling to see his wife each day.

The Royal Victoria was as much our home as it was a hospital. Built on the banks of Southampton Water, it was, in reality, a large village. The site housed an electricity generating station, a gasworks, its own reservoir, staff quarters, the school I attended, and stables, plus a bakery and a prison. Added to these was the luxury of a seawater swimming pool, filled from the estuary via the mechanics of a windmill. There was also a substantial officer's mess, as you might expect in a prestigious military building project for which Queen Victoria had laid the Welsh granite foundation stone.

If Victoria was a fan, her Prime Minister, Lord Palmerston, was not. He castigated the project, announcing that:

'the comfort and recovery of the patients has been sacrificed to the vanity of the architect, whose sole object has been to make a building which should cut a dash when looked at from the Southampton River . . . Pray, therefore, stop all further progress.'

Although his plea was ignored, he was right. While the hospital served a very valuable function in two world wars and other British battles overseas, its design seems to have been drawn up to win prizes. It was a palace of overdone exterior grandeur hiding horror and pain on three floors. It stretched a quarter of a mile from one extremity of its decorative brick wing to its central tower and on to the far reaches of another equally impressive decorative brick wing. Think of the poor orderly given orders to retrieve something from the opposite end of the hospital. A half mile round trip was possible. Apparently, the Americans used jeeps to get to distant wards when they were in residence!

The hospital had many claims to fame – not least for being Britain's largest military hospital. A bewildered Wilfred Owen, the First World War poet, was treated for shell shock there. A teenage Noel Coward performed Charley's Aunt, though I am not sure what part he played. And perhaps most intriguing of all, Dr John Watson, aide to Sherlock Holmes, revealed that:

'In the year 1878 I took my degree of Doctor of Medicine of the University of London, and proceeded to Netley to go through the course prescribed for surgeons in the army.'

How (speaking as a great lover of murder mysteries) things may have been different for us all if he hadn't!

*****

'Settling' at Netley had come on the back of a very unsettling time for me. After the war we had lived in a number of places in the UK. Then we had sailed to Singapore, arriving in August 1947, before moving onto Hong Kong. In December, due to my Mum's ill health, we had been bundled into an aircraft to get us back to Britain on compassionate leave as quickly as possible. In next to no time we were on another ship, heading for Singapore and Hong Kong again. This thirteen-month merry-go-round of travel had only come to an end when my Dad was posted home in the summer of 1948.

Needless to say, back in Britain permanently, my mother's illness remained an issue. It can only have been a matter of months, perhaps a year, after we returned from Asia that our family situation became too difficult for my father to handle. Jean and I were trundled off to a local council care home. This was a nightmare. The female staff were not kind. On arrival Jean was taken to the toddlers' rooms. I, being older, was housed in the children's section. I have a distinct memory of sitting with my back to the heavy wooden door that separated us, hearing Jean crying out for me.

'Can I see my sister?' I asked.

My carer was as spiky as shark's teeth. 'There is no communication between the sections,' she declared. By which, I gathered, she meant 'no'.

It was a distressing start and didn't get any better for either of us. At night the children slept together in a big dormitory. I was still separated from Jean. In fact, I can't remember seeing her the whole time I was there.

Of course, the move meant yet another school to get used to. Before I was allowed to go, I was given a bucket of cold water and a scrubbing brush. My allotted task was to wash down the concrete steps between the ground and first floor. No soap. I have no idea why this was necessary every day – or why it was thought a suitable job for a child, but all the children were made to work.

Thankfully, this stay did not last too long. When my Dad came to visit, he must have seen the situation for what it was. He promptly took us home again. Determined to do his best for us, he sought the advice of a Mr W. Hitchcock and under his guidance we did fare better.

Mr W. Hitchcock was a man with contacts. He was what was called an 'Army Scripture Reader'. Quaint as that may sound, The Soldiers' and Airmen's Scripture Readers Association (SASRA) has been around for two hundred years and still exists today. Its members were Christian ex-military men; evangelists, missionaries if you like, to the forces, charged with ensuring the spiritual well-being of soldiers and airmen.

Oddly, I have not been able to discover what the 'W' stands for. Walter? Wilfred? William? He is only ever referred to as 'Mr W', even at the end of an article he himself wrote. However, I do have a picture of him. He is wearing the exact same design of circular spectacles that my father had, carries a small black attaché case, and is several inches taller than his co-worker, a Mr C. H. Robertson – with no clue as to his Christian names either. Since he and Mr Robertson are wearing much the same outfit – black shoes and black trousers, white shirt and tie, a long overcoat, hat and black gloves – I do wonder if this was their 'uniform'.

Mr Hitchcock, the onetime splendidly entitled 'Misses Perks' Memorial Missioner', was the scripture reader for Gosport and no doubt had much to occupy him with the Southampton docks and Royal Victoria Hospital on his patch. Quite whether my father sought him out or Mr W offered to help I don't know, but suffice to say Mr Hitchcock played a significant part in my life. It is odd to think that without him I would not have met my husband!

His first suggestion was that Jean and I were taken in by a Christian family in Birkenhead. The father was out of work. Fostering two children was an opportunity to boost the family's finances. Mr and Mrs Heap had six children of their own, two older daughters already at work, four still in school. Having two more, Jean and I, in the house clearly didn't faze them. This time Jean and I shared a bedroom. I have vague memories of shared mealtimes but little else, other than school – yet another institution in which I sat at the back of the class, clearly not a priority as a child in care.

I was only there for three months. In the spring of 1950, the Heaps decided to keep Jean and let me go. I find it difficult to believe that I caused them any trouble. I tried hard to be good, afraid to do anything wrong. If I was late – even just a short minute – I was liable to leap into a panic. Or perhaps Mr Hitchcock's contacts found Geoff and Vi Pearson and suggested them as a better option for me, given how crowded the Heaps' household was. Certainly, I would be a lot nearer to Southampton. As it turned out, while leaving Jean was hard, finding the Pearsons was probably the best thing that had happened to me in a long while.

However, Mr Hitchcock had one more suggestion that he followed up on my father's behalf. This was a place in a children's home in Bristol – potentially a more permanent arrangement, where Jean and I would be cared for together for a number of years, not months.

I will come to that, of course. But I thought you might like to know first about where my mother and father met and why I ended up living in a drawer in a prison.

Chapter 3

Elizabeth's Story

In a BBC broadcast Winston Churchill once said that what happens in Russia is '…a riddle wrapped in a mystery inside an enigma'. I feel much the same way about my mother's story. I was so young when she forgot who I was that I learned very little about her early life. Later, my father filled in a few gaps, but I wish I had found out a lot more, especially now as I write about her.

Mum had the good fortune to be born just after Germany and Russia had signed a peace treaty to end their First World War. She had the severe misfortune to be born in the midst of a calamitous civil war. A year earlier, in 1917, the faltering dynasty of Tsars had been overthrown. The Bolsheviks, Communists led by Lenin, emerged as the pre-eminent power. A battle began, pitching the new government's Red Army into conflict with a mixed alliance of opponents – the so-called 'Whites'.

My mother's parents were White Russians and on the wrong end of defeat as the Communists hammered their way from St Petersburg to Vladivostok and to victory five years later. My grandfather, Anatoly Alexander Borisoff, was a school teacher in the small town of Verkneudinsk (now Ulan-Ude), one of the stops on the Trans-Siberian Railway. This lies in a valley at the meeting of two rivers and it is near enough to China and Mongolia to appeal to traders. In reality, it looks like the middle of nowhere. It must have been a tough place to live. The summers are generally wet, the winters icy. In January the temperatures can tumble to minus thirty degrees, sometimes as freezing as fifty below. Harsh, you would have to say, at the best of times. And this was certainly not the best of times.

When my Mum, Elizabeth Anatole Borisoff, was born in September 1918, there were White Army troops in the town, perhaps bringing some security to the family. Two years later the Communists overran the place and life must have become very difficult. Anarchy was not far behind the revolution. There were complaints about commissars – officials – who got drunk, raped women, and went about firing off guns. Across the country there was a backlash against the rich and those in authority. Looting, official confiscations or plain theft, was rampant. Lumped together with the landowners, ruling classes, and White Army officers, anyone with an education was the enemy. As a relatively well-off school teacher, my grandfather was one of 'them', not 'us', fair game for plunder.

Added to this was a famine when Elizabeth was two. This was exacerbated by the ongoing fighting and the inefficiencies of rationing under the new regime. As food supplies became scarce, desperation drove people to steal fences and furniture and to fell trees for fuel. Millions died from disease and starvation.

Remarkably, in spite of the crisis and fears of reprisals, there was still space for a joke at the government's expense. A story went around that when a teacher asked his class:

'Jesus fed five thousand people with five loaves and two fishes. What is this called?'

A pupil replied, 'The ration system.'

Somehow, Anatoly and his wife, Eugenia, kept their family of two small children together. Elizabeth had a brother, Leo, two years older than herself. Leo was adopted – the illegitimate son of a courtier, he said – though I have no idea why in such circumstances my grandparents took on another child. Leo was not born in Verkneudinsk but intriguingly, like Elizabeth, took his middle name from his adopted father. Who knows what Russian sensitivities were being circumnavigated!

What happened next is also not clear. My best guess is that the family did not join the first great exodus of White

Russians, who left the country in droves after the revolution. Many headed east, possibly keeping ahead of the advance of the Red Army, and crossed the border into China for safety. Cities like Harbin and Shanghai were favourite places to settle. However, when the Chinese government changed the rules on recognising Russian citizenship, the refugees suddenly found themselves stateless, unless they aligned themselves with the government they had escaped. Interestingly, twenty years later, when Leo filled in an official form for the British government, he stated that he and his parents were all of 'No Nationality'. Elizabeth, on the other hand, is described as Russian on her marriage certificate, although I cannot believe she was enamoured with the Communist regime in any way.

Whether wise or foolish the Borisoffs apparently sat out the civil war and as the 1920s progressed, the country stabilised and things improved. Teachers, like Anatoly, were needed if the nation was to find its feet. Unfortunately, this was simply a lull in the storm. When Stalin took control of the country, there was more chaos and bloodshed to come. Thankfully, by this time, the family had left Verkneudinsk and Siberia behind.

Elizabeth's passport says that she had a scar over her right eye. It was, in fact, a scar that ran tightly across the top of her head, from the front to the back of her skull; a distinct line where her hair did not grow. For years I had no idea what had caused this. Then, after my mother had been permanently confined to a psychiatric unit, my father found her family living in Australia. He came back with an horrific story.

I am not sure of the detail and I can only assume that Elizabeth was perhaps twelve or thirteen at the time. Clearly, the family were under threat. Local villages were being raided. Men were being killed. Girls were being raped. Eugenia, fearing for her daughter, decided that Elizabeth was better dead than abused. She took an iron bar and struck my mother across the head. Elizabeth was knocked unconscious, an ugly ribbon of blood rapidly dyeing her dark hair red.

Miraculously, you may say, my mother survived. However, she would never talk about it. Despite my Dad's questions, she refused to say what had happened to her. Justifiably, I think. Knowing that her mother had tried to murder her, for whatever reason, can never have been easy for her to bear.

Perhaps it was the threat to the family and the tragedy of this incident that brought about the Borisoffs' flight from Verkneudinsk, armed with a wad of five hundred rouble notes as bribes. That journey is definitely an enigma wrapped in a riddle. Did they make a bolt for the Mongolian border just a hundred miles or so away? Or take the train to Harbin? Or did they flee to Vladivostok and find a ship heading out of their homeland?

All I know is that Leo was in Hong Kong at the beginning of 1935 and stateless. He was nineteen and joining the Hong Kong Police. There is a splendid photograph of him, a fresh-faced teenager in his new uniform, with his service number, E27, emblazoned on his collar. His career choice is not a great mystery. A number of the White Russian youths – E Group – had already joined up to create an armed anti-piracy unit, escorting boats and ships in the seas around Hong Kong and as far away as Shanghai. Leo was recruited to replace someone who had been dismissed. What is surprising is that he didn't need to become a British citizen to do so, but then a good number of his police colleagues were Indian, local Chinese or from Mainland China – all neatly segregated into letter groups; Group A being the colonial British and Europeans, of course.

What happened to my grandparents is hard to work out. My scanty knowledge suggests that they sailed straight for Australia, settling in the Blue Mountains outside Sydney. However, it is difficult to believe that they left both Leo and Elizabeth, now in her mid-teens, to forge a new life in Hong

Kong alone. So, perhaps they lived in Hong Kong for a number of years, using their contacts in the White Russian community to find accommodation and work.

When Leo and Elizabeth were in Hong Kong, there were just a few hundred White Russians living there, but at least they were part of a close-knit community of people facing the same problems as themselves. At first, these émigrés were amongst the poorer citizens of the colony. Being stateless, they and their compatriots were not necessarily well regarded by the British. Nevertheless, most of them seem to have made something of their lives.

Some Russians opened restaurants serving cheap dishes of *borscht* and *shashlik*. Others ran grocers' shops or set themselves up as tailors. Ex-White Army men got jobs as security guards or riding instructors. One at least was a talented musician and found employment with an orchestra playing in hotels. The arrival in Hong Kong of a Russian Orthodox priest added a strong religious element to the community. I am sure this bolstered their sense of identity, which in turn brought them more security and wealth.

Tantalisingly, I have a photo of a middle-aged man in a flat cap with a bicycle – perhaps Anatoly – standing outside a food store with the name Borisoff in letters a foot high above the door. In the window there is an advert for Colman's mustard and what could be Sandeman's sherry. It is difficult to say if this is a shop in Hong Kong or Australia. However, attached to the door frame is a little metal number plate. The property number '8' is clear. Around it there are tiny symbols which could be Chinese characters. So perhaps Anatoly traded in his schoolmaster's hat for that of a Hong Kong storekeeper?

Five years after Leo joined the police, Elizabeth was living on a cul-de-sac, Hillwood Road, in Kowloon, across the harbour from Hong Kong Island. These days it is a busy backstreet of shops and flats, a little lost amongst crowded street after crowded street. In 1940 there were far more spacious colonial residences lining the local roads.

Hillwood itself lay beneath the eye of the Observatory on one side of the road, with two and three storey apartment blocks along the other.

Like many women waiting to be married, twenty-one-year-old Elizabeth did have a job. She was a masseur. Opposite the end of Hillwood Road lay the deceptively reassuring sight of the acres of the Whitfield British Army Barracks. So, perhaps it was her work or maybe it was the closeness of the army barracks to her home that did it. One way or another, Elizabeth found herself a husband. Or did he find her? Another small mystery that I will always wonder about.

Chapter 4

Alfred, Elizabeth and Me

Five months after Leo Borisoff had signed up to serve with the Hong Kong Police, his future brother-in-law, my father, was standing in front of a Major Willey being questioned about why he wanted to join the army. Alfred was twenty-one and 'taking King George the Fifth's shilling', signing up for twelve years – seven years in the regular forces, five with the reserves.

Alfred had come down to the Central Recruiting Depot at Great Scotland Yard in London a few days earlier. This, I am certain, must have been his first visit to the capital and quite a venture for him. Major Willey had ensured he was put through his paces for his fitness test. That completed, Alfred was now answering the major's basic questions without problem and adding his signature to the forms.

It was obviously my Dad's intention to join the Royal Army Medical Corps. However, it is difficult to know exactly where this desire came from. He had no previous army experience and, as far as I know, had never had medical training of any sort. At the time he was working as a barman. Before that he had been a warehouse assistant for four years. As I have mentioned, he was a very caring person, but perhaps his determination to help others as a career came from nursing his mother. He was only in his teens when she became seriously ill.

In 1935 the family home was on Spencer Street in Mansfield; a narrow two-bedroomed house, three if you assume there was no upstairs bathroom, squeezed into a terrace off the main road down to Derby. This was the house in which Alfred had been born in November 1913. He was named after his father, Alfred Rowland Taylor, who was a fitter working on the red, green and cream Mansfield trams. Alfred was possibly the eldest child in the family, though he may have been beaten to that honour by a few minutes and his twin, Richard. Sadly, Richard didn't survive for more than a few weeks and in the new year his father and his mother, Ethel, had to record his death.

I am not sure what my grandfather Alfred did in the First World War, though aged twenty-three in 1914 it is difficult to believe he wasn't called up. The conflict certainly seems to have disrupted family life; my father's sister, Marjorie, wasn't born until June 1918. After that, children came at more or less regular intervals until Alfred was ten years old. Now there were two adults, four boys and two girls crammed into their tiny house. Not that this would have been so unusual at the time.

It was while Alfred was working at the warehouse that his mother died. She was only forty-one and Kenneth, the youngest child, was six years old. If my father is to be believed, the childcare was thrust upon him. Father Alfred had better employment. Marjorie, the more likely candidate for maintaining the household, being twelve, would still have been at school. Alma, the next in line for 'women's work', was only eight and was sent to live with her grandmother. It is doubtful that Eric and George, her older brothers, were considered competent for the role. With his gentle nature I am sure my Dad did a good job, but it must have weighed on him, a young man thinking about his own prospects and no doubt wondering how and when he was to find a wife, family and life of his own.

Maybe this was the reason the army seemed an attractive proposition. It would take him away from a crowded household and teach him some valuable skills that he could put to use later on. Besides, his father had found himself a lady friend and they were anxious to be married. A stepmother for the children was what was needed and presumably Constance Stevenson was glad to take on the role. Alfred was free to pursue his own ambitions.

Less than two weeks after his interview with Major Willey, Private Alfred Taylor was at his RAMC depot. He had to hope that his army career would be better distinguished that that of his Uncle John. His mother's brother had signed up, aged eighteen, in 1905. He too was a barman, but had some army experience as part of a local regiment – the quaintly named Sherwood Foresters. Like Alfred, he committed to twelve years' service, working as a driver. Twenty months later, John was in detention awaiting trial. He had deserted his post and lost his kit. In short order he was out on the streets searching for another job and with no army pension to look forward to. His discharge papers noted unceremoniously that he was 'Incorrigible & Worthless'. Not a good example to his nephew!

Alfred's first posting was at an army training camp on the edge of Church Crookham in Hampshire. In the next year or so he sailed out to Hong Kong and was set to work at the Bowen Road Medical Hospital. This was another splendid red brick, three storied building, fighting the Royal Victoria at Netley for architectural prizes and easily winning the contest for location. It was built on the slopes of The Peak on Hong Kong Island. So steep is the hill that at one time sick patients were carried up and down it in sedan chairs. My father would, no doubt, have enjoyed the great view out over the harbour and across to Kowloon, perhaps searching out the narrow needle of a church steeple that marked the corner of the street where my mother lived.

*****

On 13 August 1940, Alfred and Elizabeth got married. It was a Tuesday, not the traditional Saturday. I have just one photo of them, coming out of a church, walking past what looks like a tall wall of sandbags. Needless to say, they are looking very happy. Alfred is in his well ironed 'Blues' uniform, with his shoes impeccably polished, and his peaked army cap in hand. Elizabeth, looking impressively slim, wears a fairly simple waisted white dress, just below the knee, with matching handbag and peep-toe shoes. No bridal bouquet or bridesmaids in view, I'm sorry to say.

I have no idea which church this was. Perhaps one of the garrison churches. Although my father had declared himself a Baptist on his army application forms, I am not sure his faith was particularly strong. (Mr W. Hitchcock, the Army Scripture Reader, certainly considered him 'unconverted'.) I also don't know what the Russian Archpriest made of Elizabeth marrying a British soldier. However, I am positive that Alfred would not have wanted to join the Orthodox Church, even if he was in love!

And so, to me…

I was born in Hong Kong just less than ten months later. The maternity ward was in another impressive hospital on The Peak – Matilda Hospital, named after the wife of its benefactor. Its website describes it in dramatic terms:

> 'the trustees of [Granville Sharp's] estate decided on Mount Kellett with its airy views of the Lamma Channel and invigorating mountain breezes as the site... From the outset, Matilda assumed the character and resilience of its namesake weathering financial crises, typhoons, war and even plague – turning out extraordinary people at extraordinary times.'

Well, it did turn out me, but I am not sure I can claim to be particularly extraordinary. The times, however, were about to get very extraordinary. Regrettably, not in a good way.

Very extraordinarily, my husband, Geoff, and I were at a cricket test match fifty years later – England versus the West Indies at Lords – when we had a most unexpected encounter with the past. It was not a great time to be playing such a good team. Nevertheless, England gave the tourists more of a game than might have been expected. In the end the match was drawn, as was the series – two all – so we were happy. During the lunch break we found ourselves chatting to two men sitting next to us. One was the nephew of the other.

It was the uncle who mentioned that he lived in Hong Kong.

'Oh,' I said, 'I was born in in Hong Kong.'

At this point the nephew chipped in, 'So was I.'

Inevitably, this was a time to compare medical notes.

'I was born in Matilda Hospital on The Peak.'

'So was I. When was that?'

A delicate question for a British woman to answer. Still, I told him. 'Sunday, 8 June, 1941.'

'So was I!'

Same date, same place. It was amusing to think that fifty years before we could well have been crying in cots next to each other and that our mothers would have been swapping comments with each other as they fussed over us.

Which brings me to my name: Dominica Deirdre Danielle.

How did I get it? Well, my father is responsible. He took it upon himself to decide what I should be called. He had wanted a boy, so only had boys' names. Rather than consulting his wife, or finding a familiar family name, he for some reason got it into his head that his army colleagues would be the best resource for ideas. When he got back to the mess, he informed them of the good news of my arrival and asked them to suggest girls' names. In the end, he essentially had a lucky dip. He got the men to write their choices on slips of paper and dropped them into a military cap.

Dominica? Well, it was Sunday. And it does mean 'belonging to God', so that was appropriate for me.

Deirdre is a little harder to fathom. I was named after Deirdre of the Sorrows, an ill-fated character in an Irish legend. Inevitably, she fell to a tragic end, which I will leave you to read for yourself. In defence of whichever soldier was responsible, the lady in question was beautiful by all accounts.

Danielle, obviously, is the girl's version of Daniel. He, unlike Deirdre you will remember, did not have a tragic end, despite spending the night in a lions' den. Apparently, whoever chose it, knowing the story, just liked the name.

My father was in the dog house when he returned from registering my birth. My mother was furious! But, of the three, she must have liked Deirdre the best – ill-fated heroine or not – and thereafter that was the name I was always known by. It was only when my husband came along that things changed. Geoff had an opinion on the matter and I adopted Dee as the name everyone uses now.

Thereafter, Alfred, Elizabeth and I should have settled down to family life. But this was 1941. Europe was already at war. That conflict was expanding on all fronts as nations drew up battle lines against each other and country after country fell before Hitler's aggression. In Hong Kong people were nervous. And they had every right to be. Somewhere in the hidden corners of the colony, a couple of farmers and a barber were plotting their downfall.

Chapter 5

The Fall of Hong Kong

I am guessing that when you think about Japan joining the Second World War your first thought is Pearl Harbour – a sudden, devastating raid on the ships of the USA, all sitting like ducks at a fair, when squadron after squadron of Japanese planes, hell bent on destruction, swept across the Pacific to Hawaii. Battleships were sunk. Cruisers and destroyers badly damaged. Nearly two hundred aircraft wrecked. Around three and a half thousand dead or injured. As a result, the USA entered the fray in the Pacific and Europe.

Pearl Harbour was on the 7 December. Within hours Japan had launched attacks on half a dozen territories, Hong Kong included. This was all part of its grand plan to create a Japanese Empire: a 'New Order in Greater East Asia'. Within a matter of months, Japan controlled territory from the northerly tip of the Kuril Islands to the southernmost trough of Indonesia, five thousand miles away.

If Pearl Harbour shocked the USA, in Hong Kong things were a little different. In the 1930s Japan had occupied large areas of east China. By 1941 its troops were perched on Hong Kong's border, looking across the colony's rural New Territories towards the city riches of Kowloon and prosperous Hong Kong Island. Only the fact that the British, not the Chinese, held the territory kept them at bay.

A hundred years earlier Lord Palmerston – yes, him again – had described Hong Kong as 'a barren island with hardly a house upon it'. This was a withering opinion to say the least, but the reality was that under British rule this very small corner of China had become enormously attractive – boasting a busy natural harbour between mainland Kowloon and Hong Kong Island, an airport, and a railway running from Kowloon, through its New Territories, to the major Chinese city of Guangzhou. Now Britain was preoccupied with Germany's aggression, Hong Kong, looking very smartly dressed indeed, was well aware that Japan was breathing down its collar.

For months prior to December 1941, there had been much discussion as to how to handle the threat Japan posed. There were regular British troops in residence, their strength stiffened by Canadian and Indian soldiers. Numbers in the Hong Kong Volunteer Defence Force were bolstered. Shelters in tunnels were constructed. Air-raid drills were practised. Hospitals prepared for the treatment of mass casualties. British women and children were advised to leave, taking ships to Australia, although perversely many chose not to go. Thirty-six hours before Japan attacked the vast majority of merchant ships fled Hong Kong Harbour and a few well-placed individuals headed for a convenient exit.

I have wondered how Elizabeth and Albert dealt with all this. Albert was, of course, tied to his army duties and, as a private, had little say in his situation. There could be no escape for him. I am sure Elizabeth, with her childhood experiences of civil war, was well aware of the family's vulnerability. Perhaps, however, they consoled themselves with the great lies that the hierarchy and local population told themselves. Japan was an inferior foe. Hong Kong would not fall. So, maybe, as my mother rocked me, her baby, to sleep each night at our home on The Peak, she believed that we were safe. That the terrors she had experienced would not threaten me.

Such optimism was sadly misguided. In reality, Japan was well prepared for war. It had a plan of action. Gathering military intelligence in Hong Kong was no problem. A number of very polite Japanese moved into the colony and set up shop – in the barber's case literally. An English-speaking general and a brigadier became farmers and enjoyed drinks in a local army mess. The Japanese Press Club overlooked the naval dockyards. Who would fail to notice the defence positions and tank traps on the main road running from the border, through the New Territories, down to Kowloon? Who could miss the fact that Hong Kong's guardians were pointing all their big guns out to sea?

If you are interested in the seventeen-day battle for Hong Kong, I will leave you to read the accounts of better qualified authors. It is enough to tell you that it began early morning with a raid on the airport and attacks across the fields and hills of the New Territories. Within a few days Kowloon was occupied, a peace envoy had been rejected, and the British troops had retreated across the water to Hong Kong Island.

This was when Albert and Elizabeth would have experienced the full force of the fighting. Barrel-loads of bombs were launched at the island's defences. Shells screamed overhead almost continuously, shattering civilian and military targets alike. In the bay they would have seen the Japanese soldiers loaded into barges, crossing the narrow harbour straits, so confident that they would not be attacked by the silenced gun positions that they played western songs to the waiting troops. Then the final battle began in earnest as the Japanese stormed ridges, secured positions, and attacked the military emplacements on Hong Kong Island from land, sea and air.

No doubt my father was at the Bowen Road Hospital, overrun with the wounded and dying, much of, if not all, the time. Where my Mum sheltered me, I do not know. Suffice to say, we all survived that fierce onslaught, until on 'Black' Christmas Day the noise of combat ceased. The unthinkable had happened. Hong Kong had surrendered. There was peace on earth; but at a bitter price – the loss of thousands of lives, military and civilian, in a war that Britain could never have won.

What followed was both bizarre and tragic. The Japanese may have had a plan to beat the British, but apparently they had given little forethought as to what to do with their captive population once they were defeated. The territory was left in limbo. The banks and shops were closed for business. Money was hard to come by. In the uneasy truce individuals began to venture out onto the deserted streets, desperate to secure food. Looting, de-looting and re-looting became commonplace. Japanese soldiers, with their khaki uniforms, quiet rubber-soled shoes, and what seemed a surprising number of gold-filled teeth, loitered in waiting, politely ambushing anyone with watches on show.

Life became very precarious. The Japanese treated the Chinese abominably. Atrocities were committed in the open for all to see. Westerners were by no means excluded. Three of Alfred's RAMC colleagues, escorting a woman back to her home, were murdered by the side of the road, while the woman herself suffered a humiliating search and had her jewellery stolen. This was by no means the worst of it. The barbarism committed is not something to dwell on here, but it is a key part of any telling of the Japanese occupation of Hong Kong. Many, including myself – even though my memories of the Second World War are naturally few – learnt an inherent loathing, even hate, of the Japanese. Something which I did not face up to until fifty years later.

*****

On 30 December Alfred and Elizabeth were separated. Military personnel were ordered down to the Murray Barracks on Hong Kong Island. Soldiers were instructed to take what they could carry and then herded the half mile down to the waterfront and onto the Star Ferry. On Kowloon side a slow procession stumbled up the main road, past the Whitfield Barracks and the end of the road where Elizabeth had lived, watched every step of the way by the locals; a laborious five-mile trek on a circuitous route to the gates of another military camp – Shamshuipo. It was, as one soldier reported afterwards, a humiliating experience for a defeated army; one made worse by their lack of food, exhaustion and injury from the fighting, and being weighed down with the need to carry as much into captivity as possible.

In my mind's eye I can see my Dad joining the queues at the ferry, pulling his belongings together as he stepped onto the Kowloon shore, staring into the faces of those lining the streets, hoping for encouragement from someone he knew, and then wearily walking into Shamshuipo and feeling that his world had been left at the gates. He was now officially a Prisoner of War. He would not see Elizabeth and me for three and a half years.

Our turn came a few days later. There was an order to meet at the Murray Parade Ground, opposite the barracks. This time the participants were civilians. My mother and I must be there at 9.30 a.m. and bring an overnight bag. There was no indication as to where we were headed, nor for how long.

In some ways my mother was unfortunate. Russia was not at war with Japan – and would not be until the final few days of the Second World War. But she was now the wife of a British soldier and had a British passport. Her brother, Leo, was a member of the Hong Kong Police and by this time had secured British naturalisation. Both were required to attend the roundup of civilians. If, as I suspect, Elizabeth and Leo's parents were still in Hong Kong, then as stateless Russians, they were free to come and go as they pleased – though life outside the internment camps was by no means easy.

Up to fifteen hundred American, British and Dutch nationals turned up at the parade ground. Chaos reigned as the Japanese tried to register everyone. There were families (whole or in part). There were couples. There were singles. There were enough children and babies to distract everyone. For cultural reasons questions on remote branches of family trees needed answering. I have some doubt as to whether Elizabeth knew who Alfred's brothers and sisters were, let alone his grandmothers' maiden names!

When this scheme proved impossible, groups were formed and then people were lined up with the tallest on the right down to the shortest on the left. There was more mayhem as small children wailed at being separated from their parents. Finally, registration was abandoned. The whole tribe of unfortunates was pulled and pushed into a pretence of order and 'marched' off the parade ground.

It was, inevitably, a far more peculiar procession than the one of soldiers that had passed that way a few days earlier. It was January and some were padded up with as much clothing as could be layered on top of other layers. Others had barely enough clothing left for the day or had borrowed ill-fitting garments. The richly-dressed rubbed neatly turned out shoulders with the ragtag and bobtail. Useful kitchen utensils were tied to bodies and teddy bears stuffed under armpits.

My mother had grabbed together what she could, but her chief concern was obviously me. With no possibility of taking a pram, carrying me on one arm, a small case, packed mainly with baby stuff, was all she could manage. She had little or nothing for herself; a few clothes, no bedding. I would like to think that someone helped her, but this was a difficult day for everyone.

As this curious jumble sale of humanity walked down towards the waterfront, the baggage that war brings was evident. Roads were pitted with holes where shells had exploded. Buildings were scarred with the blast damage of bombs. Glass and debris littered the pavements. Burnt out vehicles completed the horror show. Once again, the local Chinese turned out to watch this unusual sight; some genuinely upset to see their former friends and employers shuffling along in such a motley company.

Our destination was not so far from Murray Barracks. We were headed for the red-light end of town, poor streets of dilapidated 'hotels', which had long since lost their way. As each group arrived at the next building on the list, they stumbled up darkened stairs to dark corridors because the electricity was still out and were pressed into tiny cubicles that passed as rooms. There was no consideration as to whether anyone knew anyone else, nor which sexes would be sharing the space.

Leo ended up in the Mee Chow Hotel on De Voeux Road, blessed with a room with just one other Russian, another police officer. My mother and I were less fortunate. We were a street block away in the Stag Hotel – 'a Chinese brothel of the third class', whatever that means! We were, it seems, with three other women; two married, one single. I do wonder whether they considered themselves blessed to be sharing with a seven-month-old baby. I can only apologise very belatedly to Mrs Evans, Mrs Prichard and Miss Loureiro for their disturbed nights...

Chapter 6

The Girl in a Drawer

The Stag Hotel was a rat-infested fleapit of a place and it smelt vile. There was one bathroom per floor and it was a case of waiting well in advance, rather than when the need arose. And it must have been a quite a queue. There were at least fifty people on our floor, while another inmate downstairs reckoned there were nearly a hundred on his.

The bedrooms were at best pocket-sized. They contained a couple of chairs, a Chinese-style bed and an unwashed washbasin. Sleep was either achieved in turns or by sitting bolt upright in a line – hardly fun with a lot of grubby strangers. To add to the considerable discomfort the early mornings were disturbed by the squeals of dogs being slaughtered in the restaurant on the ground floor.

If the conditions weren't enough to send my mother into agonies of anxiety over my well-being, the food supplied certainly was. Those who had money with them were able to bribe the Chinese and Indian guards to bring them something palatable. For the rest there was just a single bowl of rice per person each day. My Mum was caught between the prospect of no longer being able to breastfeed and trying to wean me on dry lumpy rice. Once there was talk of duck soup being on the menu, but it turned out to be a revolting liquid poured over the 'meal', more likely to leave people feeling ill than well fed.

My mother suffered the indignities and deprivations of this situation for more than two weeks. Finally, the order was given to move. Everyone must gather up their meagre belongings and join the straggle of internees crowding the street below. There was a short but particularly unpleasant trek to the waterfront. Along the route the Japanese showed their sickening cruelty by beating a number of Chinese to death; acts calculated to unnerve those watching, which also served to increase the already deep loathing of their captors.

This trudge came to an end at the steamship wharf from which ships normally sailed to the Portuguese colony of Macao. After an hour or so of milling around, a higgledy-piggledy search for maps, radios or weapons in bags and boxes, pouches and pockets was abandoned as impossible. Everyone was ordered to board the waiting tugs and launches. Inevitably, there was not enough space. The boats quickly became both overloaded and top heavy. We have to be thankful that the seas were calm, the weather warm, and that the boats could hug the coast of Hong Kong Island. You may have expected the internees to have enjoyed the fresh air and freedom of the open water for a short while after their confinement in the hotels, but clearly not everyone enjoyed it. One woman described it as two hours of sweating and bad temper.

These two hours came to an end at a small jetty on the south of the island, at a place named Stanley – itself named after Lord Stanley, a British worthy, who became Prime Minister (three times it has to be said – though never for very long). This was not an unattractive location; a slim peninsula of small rocky hills with bays and beaches on either side. It does, however, suffer from chill winds in the winter and the trials of the stifling summer sun.

Despite the Japanese lack of forethought about imprisoning nearly three thousand internees, the choice of this site was not without logic. Being surrounded by sea, there was less opportunity for escape. Exit from the peninsula was more easily controlled. To the south there was a sizeable prison and beyond that a fort, part of the island's defences. Between these and the main island there was also ready-made accommodation, kitchens and other facilities belonging to St Stephen's College, a school for the sons of more wealthy Chinese.

Our boats anchored in Stanley Bay and people were transferred to junks to make shore. The walk up the hill from the jetty to the college campus must have been depressing to say the least. Gangs of frightened Chinese labourers were installing fences of coiled barbed wire around the camp. To the left was a cemetery and the disturbing sight of freshly dug graves. Ahead and stretching away to the right were the imposing white walls of the prison.

An advance party had been instructed to allocate accommodation to the internees. The smaller number of Americans and Dutch were quickly assigned their quarters. However, the crowd of British who arrived was far larger than had been allowed for. This threw any plans to house them into complete disorder. In desperation to resolve the dilemma the Brits were ordered to sort themselves out.

Chaos ensued!

Forget queuing. The more sprightly and more selfish set off in pursuit of the best rooms on offer. Possession was definitely nine-tenths of any law they could envisage being in operation. People swarmed up stairwells and along corridors and onto balconies in search of space. Those who arrived first stood in doorways to bar entrance to anyone else. Families plonked themselves in the different rooms of flats – father in one room, mother in another, and whatever children they had with them staking a claim to a bedroom or two. They were triumphant, gloating at those less nimble and less determined who were left with nothing. Until the Japanese turned up that is and began pushing everyone into rooms willy-nilly. One way or another everyone had to be accommodated.

It goes without saying that again little thought was given to who may be living with whom. People were forced to share regardless of their sex, marital status or age. Privacy became a luxury. Sadly, the selfishness that was evident in that first charge for accommodation never really went away.

My Mum found a room in Block A3, one of three buildings on the east side of the campus, close to the prison gates. The Americans occupied these apartments before the vast majority of them were repatriated in June 1942 – hence the names 'A1, A2, A3', and the thoroughfare outside becoming known as Roosevelt Avenue. Down the road were the European Warders' Quarters – thereafter called the 'Married Quarters'. Here thirty people were squeezed into spaces built for a single family. In some rooms there were as many as ten folks to accommodate. We faced much the same overcrowding in our block.

I have no idea who else was in our room, but I do know that when my mother arrived there was a chest of drawers against one wall. Seeing her opportunity, she grabbed the bottom drawer and promptly pushed me into it. This was now my drawer. Possession was one hundred percent of the law as far as she was concerned. Nobody was going to take it off us. This was to become my bed, my play area, my home.

By late afternoon on 21 January 1942 the first meal had arrived and been distributed at Stanley Civilian Internment Camp; some rice, a little fish and boiled lettuce. No doubt it was welcome, but, like most of the meals that were to follow, it was barely adequate for people who were already starving. As night fell my mother settled me to sleep and then lay down on the concrete floor beside my drawer, pulled what clothing she had around her, and waited for the cold light of a bleak future.

Chapter 7

Long Queues, Poor Stews

My overriding memory of Stanley camp is one of fear. As a two and three-year-old, I can remember having to rush to roll call – instigated twice a day, 8 a.m. and 10 p.m. after a few internees made successful escapes. We mustn't be late or my mother may be punished with a beating or a slap across her face.

Mealtimes were particularly stressful. We were fortunate to have kitchens across the road from our block, but we still had to scurry to join the queues that snaked back from the kitchen tables like interminable tails. Internees inched slowly forward, while more and more people hurried to join the line. We were hopeful that we would get a good turn. We were fearful that the food would have run out before we made it to the head of the queue.

Not only did we have to wait in line for food, we also had to form a crocodile to wash up in cold water whatever we were using for plates and cutlery. Then there was another line if we wanted a cup of hot water and yet another for any rations that were on offer. In fact, I would go as far as to say that my earliest memory is simply of being in a queue. Is it a wonder I feel British?

I also have another abiding memory – being hungry.

Hong Kong mainly lived off imported food, whether it be rice and pork from China, flour from Australia, or beef which was sailed in from Scotland. Inevitably, there was going to be a problem meeting the needs both inside and outside the internment camps. Added to this was the issue of inflation. The Japanese Military Yen replaced the Hong Kong dollar, but it was quickly devalued. Before the war a pound of rice cost the equivalent of fourteen yen (cents). By

1944 it was up to twenty yen a pound, nearly one hundred and fifty times the price.

Clearly what cash was available in the camp was never going to match inflation. Bartering became a necessity. Gold and diamonds, watches and cigarette cases, even fountain pens, became the means of securing food. A regular black market was soon in operation. Those with significant wealth on them fared well enough. Others borrowed on IOUs, to be repaid at the end of the war. It is a measure of how desperate we were that my mother told me she sold her wedding ring to buy an egg.

Our daily diet was meagre. We had a thin rice gruel for breakfast. Our other two meals in the day consisted of a small bowl of rice with a few scoops of watery stew dribbled on top. The stew was made from whatever the Japanese supplied on a particular day – a bit of meat, usually water-buffalo, maybe some fish, conger eel or later a dried salted fish, possibly vegetables. Bread was not provided, but flour was brought in which could be made into dumplings, noodles and pancakes. It also helped once people worked out how to grow yeast and the best ways to bake. Salt was not available until permission was given to cross beyond the barbed wire and use sea water to obtain it.

The quality of the food given to us by the Japanese was exceedingly poor. At first the rice wasn't too bad, but in time it became increasingly dirty and contained a lot of dust and mud, with the droppings of cockroaches and rats mixed in for measure. The meat and fish clung to a large proportion of bone and it was not unknown for the whole day's supply to be spoiled beyond edibility. Even the vegetables could be rotted or sodden on arrival.

Towards the end of the war, as Japan's supply lines were disrupted, things became considerably worse. The internees went without a proper meat ration and bread for a year. The firewood for cooking became considerably harder to get hold of. Some people resorted to burning grass. When the Americans bombed Hong Kong and destroyed the oil stocks, our electricity supplies were also cut. This stilled the pumps at the waterworks, thereby reducing our water supply. Weight loss and malnutrition were rife in the camp. I suffered alongside many others with that typical swollen belly you see in pictures of children who are severely malnourished.

There were some helps. It was possible to get parcels from relatives and friends outside the camp, even though they were facing many of the same difficulties as we were. Even so, the reality was that some received far more than they needed, whereas the vast majority got nothing. Some folk also started little gardens and supplemented their diet with the vegetables and fruit they grew. Their initiative was not always respected. Stealing did take place. Thankfully, the Red Cross provided parcels once in a while, which helped to keep us alive.

Medically, we became a desperate lot. Due to the lack of vitamins, beri-beri and pellagra were a problem. Calcium deficiency caused dental decay. Eyesight failed, another vitamin-related issue. Lack of salt in the early days brought on severe cramps. Skin infections plagued us. 'Barbed-wire disease', a psychological issue, resulted in a draining lack of initiative, loss of memory and insomnia. One of the Japanese in charge of the rations was heard to comment on his first day that the inmates looked half-washed and half-witted, as well as half-starved.

Perhaps it is appropriate here to remember that there were those who entered the camp but did not live to tell their tale. There were over one hundred and twenty deaths. The first casualty came just over a week after we arrived, the last in September 1945 after liberation. Among these were four babies and two little boys, one just older than me. Some internees were already sick. Others became ill in camp. A few had accidents from which they died. Tragically, there were a number who were killed under 'friendly fire'. Most dreadful of all, there were those tortured and executed by the Japanese on the small hill above the jetty where we had landed; shot in full view of the children and women in the camp.

If you go to Stanley today, it is possible to visit the quiet graveyard, as Geoff and I did in 1990, and see the simple memorials to all those buried there during my internment. Given the circumstances in which we were all living, it is also a tribute to the men and women who found what stones they could and provided brief inscriptions to mark the final resting places of people who deserved better.

*****

Not that everything to do with camp life was horrific. There were plenty of initiatives to make life more tolerable, particularly when it came to clothing. Some of the women had obtained hand-turned sewing machines, which had been left in one of the buildings on the camp, and so they were able to make all sorts of things, including bras! Old curtains and quilts became summer tops. Flour sacks were cut and sewn into underwear and bathing costumes, and the unravelled threads crocheted into garments and even shoes with hooks made from whittled-down wood. Before the Japanese entered Hong Kong, one factory was completing an order for a thousand pairs of shorts for scouts in South Africa. With shipping disrupted by the war, these were sent to us instead. Shorts of all sizes were carefully unsewn. Many of us ended up wearing khaki garments, their drabness relieved by skilful embroidery.

I have some good memories. One of these being allowed to go down to the beach at Tweed Bay. We had to follow the long prison wall to the cliff tops, slip through the barbed wire fence, and then negotiate a steep path down to the sand. This was no problem to me. I could simply plonk myself on my bottom and slide all the way to the beach. After the dreariness and boredom of camp life, being able to run into the sea and splash in the waves for a while was glorious. And afterwards I felt clean, which was no bad thing at all!

What comes down though had to get back up again. The climb to the camp was a real nightmare. The incline was so steep that we were reduced to making our way on our hands and knees. With time, as people became weaker, fewer felt able to make the journey and what had been a real break from the bleakness of internment was no longer possible.

Another good memory is that on our first Easter the Japanese Commandant presented all the children with duck eggs. They were large and blue, and many of us had barely seen a chicken egg in the camp at that time, let alone such a treat. This was a strange thing about our captors. They could be and were incredibly cruel to the adults. Whenever my Mum met a Japanese guard or official, no matter whether high or low rank, she must bow. If she failed to do so or committed some other minor error, it was likely that she would be assaulted. Nevertheless, the Japanese seemed to have a real soft spot for the children. They made a special allowance that milk should be provided, albeit paid for by the Red Cross. On another occasion officials of the Japanese Information Bureau handed out gifts. Mind you, this may well have been a publicity stunt because a picture of them appeared in *The Hong Kong News*.

Needless to say, the duck eggs proved a godsend. Parents were soon busy borrowing small stoves, if they didn't have one, to cook our eggs and enjoy them with us. The egg shells were not wasted either. These were ground up and fed to us to boost our calcium levels. Definitely less pleasant to consume but all in a good cause.

I was by no means short of playmates. There were around twenty-four children in my block alone and about three hundred on the site. I was one of the youngest, but there were a few dozen babies born in the camp – some to mothers already pregnant on arrival, others conceived during our internment. It is perhaps a measure of how ignorant the children were of the world beyond the barbed wire that it was possible to hear some of the older ones discussing whether they wanted to work in the kitchens or join the group who dealt with the rations when they grew up.

Oddly, as children, we had amazing freedom. The adults, by and large, were busy surviving and our parents were very exercised in looking after us as well. We roamed all over the camp, built friendships with whomever we wanted, and invented and played our own games. I like to think I didn't get into too much trouble, but others remember crawling under the boundary wire, defying the curfew with night-time escapades, having battles with mud bombs, and taking bullets to bits.

One thing I do remember clearly is amusing ourselves at the expense of our captors. Encouraged by the older children, we little ones would stand in a row and in turn go up to a Japanese guard and bow. Being polite, they were honour bound to stop what they were doing and bow in return. One of them had twenty to thirty children lined up waiting for their turn. As a result, he got into terrible trouble for not doing his job. When the camp commandant learned about our prank, he got furious with us. We were banned from playing it again.

*****

As I finished the first half of this chapter with mention of the terrible deaths of those murdered by the Japanese, it is good to remember that not all the Japanese were cruel. Several accounts of the internment at Stanley Camp pay tribute to the Revd. Kiyoshi Watanabe, a Lutheran minister, whose actions, at risk to himself, were a real witness to his Christian faith.

Kiyoshi – 'Uncle John', as some called him – was born in a village called Nanataki on Japan's southern island, Kyushu. He was raised as a Buddhist, but his elder brother, Hidezi, a medical student, gave him a Bible. Intrigued by it, as there were no local Christians, Kiyoshi persuaded his father to let him travel to a nearby city to complete his education. He attended a church, but came away with more questions than answers. Baffled, he wrote to his brother, saying that the book was a mystery to him, but reading it gave him peace. Surprisingly, Hidezi, not a Christian himself, recommended finding a Lutheran church. Here Kiyoshi got answers, made a commitment to follow Jesus, and was baptised. By the age of twenty-five, he had become a Lutheran pastor.

When war broke out Kiyoshi was in his fifties, had married, and lost two daughters to dysentery and his first wife in childbirth. Now he and his second wife, a school teacher called Mitsuko, were living at Hiroshima. His two sons were about to be called up to fight, while his three daughters remained at home. Kiyoshi was shocked to receive his own call-up – an order to enrol in the war effort as an English translator.

Kiyoshi arrived in Hong Kong in 1942. He worked first in the camp at Shamshuipo where my father was interned, then at Bowen Road Hospital, and finally in Stanley. What he saw at Shamshuipo – thin, emaciated men, half dressed and many of them clearly unwell – shocked him; as did the brutal way that Japanese soldiers beat and tortured the POWs and Chinese. He resolved to help whoever he could, in whatever way he could, without compromising his allegiance to Japan.

With the help of people outside the camp Kiyoshi began to bring in messages to POWs. He found robes for an interned Catholic priest, and pencils and paper for a colonel with a love for drawing. He organised for books to be delivered to Canadian patients at the hospital. His greatest service was almost certainly the medicines and surgical instruments he smuggled into Shamshuipo in a leather briefcase. When dysentery broke out at the camp, it was Kiyoshi that carried in serum to save some of the victims. All this was done at considerable risk to himself. If caught, he would certainly have been tortured, perhaps executed for treason, as others were. When thanked for his help, he usually retreated with a shy smile. When praised for his courage, all he would say was that it was God who did it.

Although I do not remember Kiyoshi, I must have met him. He was at our children's Christmas Carol Service in 1944. After we had sung *Away in a Manger*, he asked if he could sing. He sang *Holy Night* and a Japanese carol we did not know. Then he talked about how children from every nation should be together, because Jesus is the same for everyone.

Tragically, given his kindness and humanity, when the atomic bomb fell on Hiroshima a few months later, Kiyoshi's wife, Mitsuko, and his eldest daughter, Miwa, were among the tens of thousands who died.

Chapter 8

Life on the Inside

Looking back, it is strange to think that this prison was my world. I was seven months when I arrived and four years old when we left. Life was lived in a drawer, queuing for food, being hungry, sharing a room with twenty to thirty others, clinging on to whatever possessions came our way.

I am tempted to say that my mother brought me through all this single-handedly, but I suspect this isn't entirely true. No doubt she needed to forge friendships with the mothers around her. It would have been grim to share the space we had without building good relationships. There would have been some comfort in swapping nuggets of information on what to do, where to find bits and pieces, as well as perhaps caring for each other's children from time to time. One good thing was that the internees set up a kindergarten on the camp, which relieved her of some childcare and provided a natural contact with other parents.

Still, I do think it must have been extremely hard for her. She arrived with next to nothing, the wife of a low ranking orderly. She would, I am sure, have been classed as Eurasian. She had been raised in Russia and within the exiled Russian community in Kowloon. English was a second language, albeit one she spoke well. In the conceited circles of colonial Hong Kong these would have all been barriers to integrating.

There was another problem that created a great deal of ill feeling in Stanley. Crowded together like proverbial sardines, starving for the want of better food, the internees were all too aware that many of the wives and children had been given the opportunity to leave Hong Kong and had decided to stay. There was a lot of resentment amongst those who had not had the chance to get away. They were suffering a great deal more with so many women and their offspring in the camp. I don't think my mother had been given such an option, but no doubt the feelings ran high at times.

Nevertheless, there are positives to draw on. There were twenty to thirty Russians in the camp. With such a small community of her countrymen and women in the colony, it is highly likely that she knew many, if not all of them. Leo was there, living alongside members of his Hong Kong Police unit. I like to think that Leo looked out for his sister. Having said that, I didn't know he was in the same camp as her until I began my research for this book. Certainly, I have no memory of being played with by 'Uncle Leo'.

There was at least one other Russian woman at Stanley – Nadia Seraphina (formerly Basargin). Like Elizabeth, she had married a British man. She was the wife of William Seraphina, from Scotland, who worked as an official with the Chinese Maritime Customs. Nadia lived in one of the bungalows on the west side. She had four children in the camp, the youngest just nine months older than me. There is very good reason to believe that the two women knew each other, as you will find out.

My mother may have found more than enough to do, keeping life and limb together and looking after me, but there were at least five or six other masseurs in the camp. These were employed at what became designated as 'Tweed Bay Hospital', a three-storied building overlooking the south of the peninsula, a few yards from where we lived. Any help the hospital staff could get must have been welcome. So, perhaps she used her skills there.

Regrettably, my Mum did have her own health issues. She developed an ear infection and with no drugs to deal with it, the problem spread to the mastoid bone behind her ear. This causes inflammation, headaches, high temperatures, and a loss of hearing. If unchecked, it can be life-threatening. The solution was to send her into Hong Kong for an operation;

clearly an emergency measure, because few people were allowed to leave the camp.

As I have said, there were complications and a facial nerve was cut, causing her great distress. Tragically, I don't think that the treatment solved the problem. The infection seems to have spread deeper into her brain. When she returned to Stanley, she took a long time to pick up. Afterwards, she began to notice that she was forgetting things. I do wonder if this was the root of the mental illness that troubled her life.

I have no idea who looked after me while she was away. Many years later, I had an encounter with a British nurse that makes me wonder if she was involved in my care. During the 1960 census I was at Bristol Royal Infirmary doing my nursing course. When I stepped up to the hospital desk, the sister behind it needed the basic details to fill out her form.

'Your surname?'

'Taylor'

'And Christian name?'

'Dominica Deirdre Danielle.'

She looked up. 'You were in Stanley Camp in Hong Kong in the war?'

'Yes...'

'I was one of the nurses who looked after you.'

I don't remember her name or what more was said, but it was a strange happenstance one way or another. Now I wish I had asked her about her time there and what she knew of my mother, but others were waiting their turn and the moment was lost.

Leo seems to have been kept busy. The Hong Kong Police certainly got themselves involved in camp life, particularly if there were risks to be taken. In the early days, it was the young police officers who raided the Japanese godowns – sheds – stuffed with food supplies. Tins of golden syrup, packets of cheese, bully beef, butter and sugar disappeared into their dormitories. Two hundred and forty pound bags of rice were hidden under their beds. Eventually, they were found out. Grains of rice were spotted on the road and the trail followed to the police accommodation. For their sins they got half rations for a week, some did a stint in the prison, and in time they were moved into new quarters, where presumably the Japanese could keep a better eye on their activities.

In an early, successful, attempt to escape from Stanley, one of the escapees was a British police superintendent. It was also four of his colleagues who made a failed escape bid soon afterwards. Unfortunately, this unhappy crew were caught a few miles from the camp. It was around a month before they were returned in a police van and incarcerated in the prison. They did not talk about their ordeal, but their bayonet wounds were clear and they showed signs of starvation.

On the much lighter side of camp life, Leo's crew involved themselves in amateur entertainment. They gave informal concerts and transformed themselves into fauns and shepherds for ballets. I like to think that it was the Russians among them who excelled at the latter!

This was by no means all. The police were signed up as woodcutters for the kitchens, a strenuous task that only the fittest could take on. Bizarrely, there is a cartoon of them drawn by one of the internees acting as 'Foster Fathers' to earn a little kudos and cigarettes. One character is washing clothes, while another hangs them on the washing line. Next to them in a handmade cart is a small child wailing for want of attention!

It seems, though there is no proof one way or the other, that Leo and Nadia Seraphina also used the time to develop more than an acquaintance. Quite how you can conduct an affair in what was essentially a severely cramped village of nearly three thousand people and expect no-one to notice I am not sure. Incongruously, the cemetery and freshly dug graves were popular for rendezvous. There is another cartoon entitled 'HK Police Playground. The Empty Grave'.

In it a young woman is being helped out of the hole by her male friend. Hardly private and you do wonder if lovers had to form a queue!

*****

The most difficult days came as the war ended. As I have mentioned, conditions deteriorated, food was scarce, the electricity and water cut-off, our sources of fuel for cooking exhausted. And, ironically, we faced a new threat to our lives. War being fought on our doorstep.

As the Japanese forces began to fall back, the Americans began air-raids over Hong Kong. It goes without saying that the sight of planes swopping in low over the island cheered everyone. They began as early as 1943, bombers passing overhead, targeting Japanese convoys who dared to venture onto our horizon.

However, on 16 January 1945 our enthusiasm for the fight was quashed. The previous day a storm of fighters had swept in over the sea. The city and harbour had been bombed from morning to afternoon. On the sixteenth the action became too close for comfort. The Japanese had guns on the prison roofs and our camp guards were ready with their rifles and revolvers as planes strafed the prison. The noise of war roared around us. Bombs dropped in the bay, shaking the buildings. Children screamed and our parents prayed that nothing would harm us as tracer bullets ripped across the ground. And then, there was an almighty explosion. A bungalow near to the cemetery had been hit. Fourteen internees were killed. The camp was in shock. After that, there was never the same exuberance for the battle for Hong Kong.

Needless to say, liberation did not finally come until August 1945 when Japan capitulated to inevitable defeat and the bombs which destroyed Hiroshima and Nagasaki. Surprisingly, there was little celebration. A strange quietness developed in the camp. The Japanese stayed in their HQ. Our guards disappeared. The police put on their uniforms and patrolled the fence perimeter. In the evening there was a thanksgiving service and we waited to be rescued.

A couple of days later visitors began to arrive. Among them were officers from Shamshuipo where Alfred had been interned. Two days after that ferry loads of emaciated, battered men arrived from the camp, marching in tattered ranks into Stanley, while wives and lovers looked on anxiously to see if their man was among them.

This is when I should have met my father again. But he was not there. He had been taken to Japan many months before and nobody knew whether he was alive or dead. My poor mother. How she must have wept.

Chapter 9

Alfred's War

It is one of the great sorrows of the Second World War that those who suffered rarely, if ever, talked about their ordeals. In part, it would have been harrowing reliving all that distress. Why would you want to do that? However, there was another factor, which I find more troubling. On their arrival in the UK my parents were told not to tell others what had happened to them. The people of Britain had been traumatised enough by their own travails. It was better not to pile on the agonies of Japanese internment, to relate the barbarity you had seen, possibly undergone yourself.

So, when it comes to my father's experiences of the war, he never spoke about what happened to him, except to say that it had been dreadful and gave him nightmares for years. It is really only through the research I have been able to do – using army archives and reading books written by others – that this chapter can tell you anything about events after he joined the officers and soldiers sweating their way down to the Star Ferry and up Kowloon's main road towards Shamshuipo POW camp on the 30 December 1941.

When my Dad arrived at the camp, the former home of the Middlesex Regiment and a battalion of Indian soldiers had been gutted. Furniture had been taken from all the barrack huts. Doors had been ripped from their posts; in some places window frames were gone as well. Electrical wiring had been stripped from the walls and ceilings. Most of the sanitary units had disappeared. Rivers of water were gushing out onto the floor where taps had been wrenched from their pipes. The spoils of war indeed!

The only thing for my Dad to do was to latch onto a few of his mates and find a space on a concrete floor – or a wooden one if he was fortunate – to bed down. The Japanese provided some rice, a few cooking containers, some sizeable gnarled tree trunks for firewood, and no tools whatsoever to chop the wood up. One of the huts was dismantled, fires started, and the rice boiled, but any thought that it was 'cooked' was wishful thinking on the cooks' part. So, for the first few days everyone ate whatever they had brought with them, what they could buy from traders over the barracks boundary (there was no fencing as yet), or what gifts Chinese friends were able to hand over. The latter were particularly courageous. They often got a beating from the Japanese guards for their kindness.

Shamshuipo was by no means as nice a location as Stanley. The barracks had been built on a tediously flat square of reclaimed land which jutted out into the wide estuary of the Pearl River. The water on two sides was dark and polluted with sewage. While there were hills to the north, to the south lay the damaged streets of the city. Stanley, with its beaches and views out over the South China Sea, was much more pleasant on the eye.

Nevertheless, Shamshuipo was a barracks with readymade accommodation laid out in neat military rows to house a few thousand soldiers. The POWs were all army men or members of the Volunteer Defence Corps. There were no women and children, whose particular needs must be catered for. Perhaps most important of all, the established hierarchy of the armed forces meant that it was clear from day one what the pecking order was. There was no need to work out who was to run what. Squads came with valuable skills and men already well trained in all sorts of practical tasks. Within a short space of time, discipline had been restored. Men were banded into their units, moved into huts together, and assigned their roles. Shamshuipo was quickly on its way to becoming a fully functioning community, while at Stanley internees tried to find out who was who, what they could do, and held elections to appoint leaders.

By the end of 1942 Shamshuipo camp had an amazing range of activities up and running. There was a store and a tool room, a tailors and a shoemakers. There were groups of brickies, fitters, plumbers and tinsmiths on hand. If you needed your watch or spectacles repairing, or even a book rebinding, a workshop would help you out. Plans were being made for a pig farm and for chickens and ducks to be brought onto the site. On the insistence of the Japanese there was even an 'Old Folks Home' for the over sixties.

My father would have been employed at the hospital established in a building on the sea front. Initially, this was no more than cobbled together with a few iron bedsteads. There were no drugs, instruments or medical supplies available other than those that the men brought in themselves. Once the work teams were in place, it was possible to install electrical wiring and piping pirated from elsewhere, construct tables from floorboards, and turn roughly drawn sketches made by doctors into equipment.

Needless to say, it took a long while for all this to be completed. Following the fighting, many of the men were in poor shape. People struggled with beri-beri, dysentery, malaria, malnutrition, pellagra and a host of other complaints. Weight loss affected everyone. After ten months, a general malaise set in. Apathy was universal. An epidemic of diphtheria raged and showed no signs of weakening. By December, one year after arriving at the camp, nearly two hundred had died. The improvements in medical facilities and the arrival of Red Cross parcels made a huge difference. Thereafter, the number of deaths each month dropped rapidly.

As at Stanley, camp life did have its amusing moments. Quite early on, before the pig farm was planned, a batch of pigs were delivered. Predictably, the animals seized the first opportunity they had to escape (albeit into the confines of a prison camp). With triumphant squeals they set off in every direction. Internees gave chase, while their colleagues doubled up in laughter at the farce unfolding in front of them. Finally, the pigs were enticed into one of the huts and bedded down for the night. That was not the end of the story. Pork on the menu was good. Having no knives to do the deed was not.

On another occasion a three-ton lorry arrived with clothing. Much needed, except the items were like the remnants that the rag and bone men don't want after a jumble sale. Mainly it was underclothing or non-essential items, such as tuxedos and dress shirts, that the Japanese had stolen from military bases and private homes. A second load proved more worthwhile. When the loads were sorted, some of the articles had name tags. These were dutifully returned to their rightful owners!

At Stanley, during the three and a half years my mother and I were interned, there were a few escapees, some internees were transferred to another site, and north and south Americans were repatriated. At Shamshuipo there was another, less attractive, route out. This was on one of the drafts of slave labour to Japan; men taken by the Japanese to bolster their war effort and to free up more of their countrymen to join the fight. The voyage to Japan was a desperate one. These boats were known as 'Hell Ships'. Prisoners could be held in cramped cargo holds, gasping for air, starved of food and water, for weeks on end.

The first boatload from Shamshuipo was an interesting one. In September 1942 six hundred and twenty inmates were rounded up and put aboard a ship heading for Japan. The Japanese guards must have been delighted. Their superiors took the opportunity to get rid of as many of the people who were causing them trouble as they could – the 'Bad Hats', as one internee called them. It is not unthinkable that many of the British officers were happy to see the back of them too.

I am glad that my father was not on that first draft and thankful that he was not on the second. The Hell Ships were always under threat of attack by Allied aircraft and submarines. When the *Lisbon Maru* left Hong Kong three weeks after the first draft, it had nearly three times as many men aboard – most of them considered to be the fittest POWs in the camp.

Just outside Shanghai the ship, unmarked as carrying POWs, was attacked by torpedoes fired from an American submarine. The crippled boat was abandoned by the Japanese, but the hatches above the holds in which the POWS were kept in appalling conditions were battened down. Not only did many of the Shamshuipo soldiers go down with the ship, but those who did escape onto the deck or into the water were shot at by the Japanese on other vessels. More than eight hundred lost their lives.

The third draft became known as the 'Propaganda Draft'. The Japanese promised a luxury liner for the thousand men and more who were selected. While the description of the boat may have been correct, it was reported afterwards that the ship was so overcrowded there was no space to lie down.

Two more Hell Ships set out in 1943, both carrying around five hundred POWs. For the first of these the Japanese decided to conduct psychology tests to decide whether 'successful' candidates would be assigned to the docks at Osaka on Japan's central island or to the coal mines of Hokkaido in the north. The candidates had a field day. Half of them proved to be colour-blind – a very high percentage for members of the British armed forces you would think! And many of them seemed unable to complete simple sums – additions, subtractions, multiplications and divisions; a lack of intelligence that would have seen them marched out of their recruitment office in short order.

My father missed out on all these drafts, but in April 1944 he was ordered to join the last draft to leave Shamshuipo. As you will have gathered from the numbers already sent to Japan, the camp had been seriously reduced in size and there was little manpower left to choose from. If the fifth draft had been scraping the barrel, this one must have been scratching around for anyone still able to swing a shovel. I don't know whether I am glad my Dad was well enough to go or obviously in such poor shape that he was one of the last two hundred to be considered suitable. One way or another his ship left a couple of weeks after Easter and he was sent to work in the docks at Osaka.

My Dad was interned in what was called Osaka no. 1 camp. I have to admit that the descriptions of the camp suggest it was totally inadequate for more than four hundred POWs. The internees were bunked in wooden huts, camouflaged with mud. There was a kitchen with eight brick stoves, a ten-foot square communal bath and less than a dozen showers. The air raid shelters were no more than a large wooden building slap bang at the centre of the camp and five smaller huts around the perimeter.

The site was located on the waterfront amongst potential military targets for American bombers. I guess it is no surprise that when the site was attacked at the end of the war, it went up in flames. The POWs were moved to another camp – which was also destroyed, although not before the POWs had been moved again. This third camp was damaged but survived long enough to get to the ceasefire.

The POWs were manual labourers. They loaded and unloaded the ships and railway wagons, worked in the warehouses, and shuttled clothing and food back and forth as ordered. Work started at eight and finished at four, with an hour at noon and breaks depending on the job they were doing. For this they received one yen a day. Each morning they got a breakfast of rice and soup, and carried a 'packed lunch' of seaweed with rice, or maybe a piece of bread, to work. Dinner, not surprisingly, was also rice and soup with one vegetable: cabbage, aubergine, onion, potato or radish. Fish was served once every ten days and meat once or twice a month. On paper it doesn't look too bad, but I am sure it was no picnic given their poor state of health. Apparently, an average of seventy men were unable to work on any given day due to illness.

One interesting fact is that there was a hospital on the camp. There were Japanese and POW doctors and medics and a POW dentist. I wonder if my father was on the medical staff, able to escape the hard labour by caring for others?

*****

When the nightmare of the Pacific War came to an end, someone was given the task of listing all the POWs in the camps across Japan and noting down their next of kin. It is clear that Alfred knew where we were during our separation. He gave Elizabeth's name and her address as the 'Internment Camp Stanley Hong Kong'. How my Dad made it to Hong Kong I do not know. I cannot find any records of that journey. However, when he did arrive, devastatingly, he discovered that my mother and I had gone. We had already been airlifted out. We had been given places on a seaplane and were seven hundred miles away in the Philippines.

Chapter 10

On the Move

I was angry.

I had summoned up all the fury that a four-year-old can manage. I was ready to explode at the wrongness of the scene I was witnessing. There was a man kissing my mother. What was worse was that my Mum was as happy to embrace him as he was her.

As far as I was concerned this had never happened before. Ever. Somehow a complete stranger had walked, run even, into our lives and was turning my topsy-turvy world the right way up.

In defence of my outburst, I don't remember my Mum talking about my Dad while we were in Stanley. Nor do I recall seeing a photo of him; my mother didn't have one to show me. Of course, I knew that children had dads. My friends had fathers; there were any number of them in the camp. In my world, however, it was just Mum and me. I had complete claim on her care and concern. To find her suddenly in someone else's arms was a shock I was going to need time to get over.

My Dad had arrived in Manila from Hong Kong on the *Empress of Australia*, a war-grey troopship now transporting soldiers and internees back to the UK. Ironically, this was a German ship. Originally, it had been named after one of the country's Grand Admirals, Alfred von Tirpitz. He had built up the German navy prior to the First World War and can best be described as belligerent when it came to Britain. Still, the ship was now being put to good use in taking two thousand people back home.

Coincidentally, this was also the boat we had been assigned to. Neither Alfred nor Elizabeth knew this. It must have been amazing to find each other on board ship. I wonder how long it took them to recognise each other. My Dad was down to six stone; my Mum had aged terribly and her pretty face was now disfigured. A mere second or two? Or did they have to peer for a while beyond their haggard appearances?

No doubt the long sea voyage helped my parents rebuild their relationship. You read sometimes of how post-war relationships went sour, because one partner's personality had been damaged by their experiences. Thankfully, this was not true of my parents. I am sure it took time, but they continued to love and care for each other. In the years afterwards, when my mother was very ill, I remember my father always being gentle and very tender towards her.

For me, the journey was a strange adventure, discovering a world I didn't know existed. The *Empress* was a lively place, as people renewed contact with friends and family, enjoyed good food, regained energy, and were entertained by bands, films, games and shows. Now and again we docked at quaysides and were allowed off the boat. We called in at Singapore, busy with navy boats. Then at Colombo in Sri Lanka, where we were given second-hand clothing. And from there to Aden; a town surrounded by unfriendly volcanic cliffs with hawks circling in the air above us.

At a port called Adabiya, close to the start of the Suez Canal, my parents were in for a treat. It was announced that people would be taking a bus ride out into the desert. A converted hangar in an army camp had been decorated in welcome. There were carpets on the floor, cushioned chairs, flags used as tablecloths, and shell cases filled with roses. An area had been fenced off as a nursery, with a swing, slide, seesaw and rocking horses. If this wasn't enough, the cakes, drinks and sandwiches supplied were all free. What more would a little girl want while her Mum and Dad looked at clothes?

It must have seemed like an oasis in the desert to my mother. In another hangar there were dressing gowns and nighties, coats and gloves and scarfs, skirts and jumpers, stockings and shoes, sets of underwear and, bless the British, corsets! Unlike the hand-me-downs of Colombo (though these were appreciated too) the garments and accessories here were all new. And, believe it or not, cosmetics were on sale. I can imagine my Mum getting back on the bus, struggling under bundles of clothing, but as happy as a child at Christmas. If there was any damper on the day, it must have been heartbreaking to see German POWs still in their grey uniforms working on the roads.

We sailed up the Suez, the canal banks littered with the tangled metal of war debris, called in at Port Said for the soldiers to fill out forms, and then stopped ever so briefly at Gibraltar to collect the post. After that life was a little less fun. A storm blew up and people being sick was the story for a couple of days. After weeks at sea, we made it to the mouth of the River Mersey – only to discover there was a dock strike on and, what with this and the gale still blowing, we would have to wait to disembark.

Nevertheless, the welcome as we entered the Liverpool docks on 27 October 1945 was very worthwhile. A ferry, packed with people waving at us, circled around the ship. On the quayside there was a crowd of people cheering. A band played songs. A general had turned up to greet us. The mayor and other worthies gave speeches. For a short while – just once in our lives – we were the nation's heroes.

Once the paper work had been completed and travel plans and tickets organised, we were allowed off the ship. People were handed chocolate and a bag of food for the journey. Tea and biscuits were served at the railway station. I am sure I must have thought Britain was the most wonderful country in the world. Sadly, it was not long before it was clear that not everyone was glad to see us.

On the Empress of Australia my parents had given an address on the outskirts of Mansfield as our contact in the

UK. This was the home of relatives of my Dad's stepmother. Our first lodgings did not go well. The husband was not happy to have us in the house. My Mum was not much of a cook. She had little or no idea about British food and what to do with it. Doing the shopping was also a great stress for her. She didn't understand the money – twelve pennies to a shilling and twenty of those to a pound; with farthings, halfpennies, thrupenny bits, sixpence pieces and half-crowns thrown in for good measure – all very different from the dollars and cents she was used to. What exactly was a ten-bob note?

To make matters worse I was a very fussy eater. There were a lot of potatoes and whatever could be found to go with them; not a grain of rice in sight. You can imagine that refusing to eat what was placed in front of me was not appreciated when everyone was trying to make do on rations. The husband was furious and said I had to eat what was put on my plate. Ignorant of the effects of malnutrition, he thought I must be overweight because of my swollen belly. By all accounts, we did not stay there for long. After that we went to live with one of my father's brothers.

In retrospect I feel we were shunted from pillar to post for the best part of two years. We lived in the Mansfield area for a while, then we moved to York. My father had chosen to stay in the army, living in the barracks there. It did seem to me that we had hardly settled before we were on the move again.

As you can imagine, I found all this difficult. I had been thrown into a new culture, in a cold country, without friends (I should have been in school and wasn't, or when I was, I was terrified because I still did not know my alphabet nor much else that was deemed important by stern teachers), and living with strangers who apparently didn't like us. The food was a real problem and I hated wearing shoes. Inevitably, in the winter I got chilblains – certainly a new complaint as far as I was concerned. Added to all this I needed to get used to a new family member. My mother had become pregnant shortly after we arrived in Britain. Now Jean, my little sister, born in August 1946, was making her presence felt wherever we went.

This unsettled existence should have come to an end in August 1947 when my Dad was posted to Bowen Road Hospital in Hong Kong and we sailed out to Singapore and then on to my 'real home' a few days later. Unfortunately, I don't think my grandparents were still living in Kowloon. Leo had sailed to Australia on *HMS Striker* after the war. As I have said, it is possible that Anatoly and Eugenia were already there. If not, it is likely that they would have gone with him or at least followed him as soon as he was settled in New South Wales.

In normal circumstances my father would have signed up for a tour of duty and we could have settled down to a comfortable climate, familiar food, and renewed old friendships. However, the week before Christmas we were back in the UK on compassionate leave. My Mum had taken unwell. The fact that the four of us were flown from Hong Kong, not put on a ship, tells you how serious her condition must have become. Remarkably, about a month later we were on our way back to Asia again. I can only think that the medics thought that a warm climate, sea air and the familiarity of Hong Kong would help my mother. If so, they were badly mistaken.

For me, these moves were good news. The growing heat of the sun as we travelled south was wonderful. I could kick off my stiff British shoes and run around the decks barefooted to my heart's content. My parents were unoccupied and available to give Jean and me their full attention. There was even a bit of a school on board the ships; enough at least to keep me interested in my education.

Not everything went to plan. On one occasion we were sailing through a terrible storm. I was sitting at the end of the table, when all the crockery headed in my direction. I can remember having to be picked out of the smashed china. Another time I was supposed to be caring for Jean. She was at the crawling stage and was just about to disappear through the ship's railing when someone caught her. The times being what they were, even though I was only six or seven years old, I got a walloping from my Dad – more in relief than anger, I expect – for not looking after her.

We were housed in Whitfield Barracks, close to my mother's old Kowloon home. My Mum wasn't well, so Jean and I had to be looked after by others. With due respect to my sister, she was a little tinker, into everything, while I was expected to be the sensible older sibling caring for her.

Any hope we would be settled was soon dashed. We arrived back in the Far East in March 1948. At the end of July, my Dad had packed all our bags and we were in Hong Kong Harbour, boarding *HMT Lancashire*, bound for Britain. This time we were not coming back. From now on, I would just have to get used to wearing shoes and eating platefuls of potatoes.

Chapter 11

Home from Home

This just about brings me back to where I started my story. Well, to where I left myself at the end of chapter 2, having returned from the Pearsons to our home at Netley.

As I have said, when my Dad was sent to the Royal Victoria Military Hospital, life continued to be as complicated as ever. Over the next few years my mother's mental health deteriorated. She became catatonic, losing her way into strange behaviour, adrift from reality in a sort of stupor. A place was found for her at an enormous, somewhat scary (from my point of view) county psychiatric institution – Park Prewett Hospital, outside Basingstoke, thirty miles away. Once there, she never returned home. We visited her, of course, but she had no idea who we were. It is a measure of how tragic my mother's life was that she stayed in Park Prewett for more than half her lifetime, dying in the summer of 1994, aged seventy-five.

After Jean and I had been in the council home, then with the Heaps, and I had lived with the Pearsons, there were a brief few months when we were a family again. However, plans were being made for Jean and me to be put into care once more. What better place could there be than a Christian institution? My father's friend, the Army Scripture Reader, Mr W. Hitchcock, knew of an orphanage on the outskirts of Bristol that could possibly take us. With my father's permission, he set about arranging for us to go into one of the children's homes founded by a Prussian pastor, George Muller.

Mr Muller was a fascinating character. His story is well worth reading, if you are not familiar with it. He is one of those Christian heroes of the past, much loved of authors and their publishers. (I have counted at least a dozen books for you to choose from!) For any preacher looking for an illustration on the power of prayer George's experiences of God's help are a wonderful resource; from the amazing – the provision of money to open and maintain several orphanages, homes to thousands of children, without appealing for funds – to the quirky – needing a mild south wind so that a boiler could be mended – to the miraculous – the dispersal of a mid-Atlantic fog, so he wasn't late for a meeting in Canada.

George was born in 1805 and was, by his own admission, an all-round bad boy. Before he was ten, he had a nice line in thieving, stealing amongst many things government money entrusted to his father, a tax collector. By fourteen he was a drunkard. At sixteen he was in prison for running up bills in hotels and then scarpering without paying. In spite of this up-to-no-good approach to life, his indulgent father wanted him to be a clergyman. George was sent to cathedral school and university. Remarkably, aged twenty and not in the least bit reformed in character, he was accepted as a candidate for the priesthood and had permission to preach in Lutheran churches.

Something had to change. A friend invited him to a private home for a Saturday evening meeting; a few people singing hymns, praying and reading the Bible. George would rather have spent the evening playing cards and drinking, but he did go. Away from the formal religion of the churches and cathedral, he was out of his depth. These Christians were different. When one of them got down on his knees to pray (not the normal Prussian way of praying), George was awestruck by the man's devotion to God. He went home with a sense of joy he had never experienced before. Shortly afterwards, the Bible verse:

> For God so loved the world that he gave his one and only Son, that whoever believes in him shall not perish but have eternal life

made a deep impression on him. In short, in spite of his many misdemeanours, he discovered that God loved him.

Two other incidents had great influence on George's life. When he informed his father that he wanted to be involved with a missionary society, his father told him that he had not spent money on his son's education to see it wasted. He was to get a secure living, so that he could support his father in his old age. In his anger at George's plans his father declared George was no longer his son. In a way, with his mother already dead, George learned what it was to be an orphan. Thankfully, there was a good end to this unhappy episode. Around nine years later, George's father confessed that he was moved by his son's faith and they were reconciled.

Around the same time that George was rejected by his father, as a poor divinity student, George got free lodging in an orphanage. The orphanage founder had relied entirely on God's provision for the finances and George was fascinated by this man's faith. So, perhaps it is not surprising that when George ended up in Bristol as a church pastor, he had the vision to start an orphanage and was determined never to ask people for funds. In 1836 he rented a terraced house and opened it up for girls. Before the end of the year a second home, just along the street, was started and a year later, another for boys. Needless to say, the neighbours weren't happy with the din of dozens of noisy orphans on their doorstep and let their feelings be known! In 1849 the orphans from four houses were moved to an area outside Bristol called Ashley Down, where Muller now has a road named after him. By 1870 there were five purpose-built orphanages on the site, housing two thousand children, all being run without appealing for money.

I am sure one of these homes was what Mr Hitchcock had in mind for Jean and me. However, the charity had another idea. Three years before they had bought a house in Minehead; a holiday home for the Bristol children. Now they were planning to use it all year round. Jean and I would be the first of a small unit of ten 'orphans'. It is clear from the paperwork that Mr Hitchcock made all the arrangements. My father was suffering from a pyloric ulcer. Both he and my mother were in hospital around the time we went to the home. There is one amusing note in Mr Hitchcock's application. He mentions that Jean and I are to be checked over by a Medical Officer, but that we are 'clean'.

On the Tuesday before Easter Jean and I and a small parcel of clothes were bundled into Mr Hitchcock's car and he drove us to our new home. Hillbury on Minehead's Martlet Road was, and still is, an imposing red-bricked house. As the car turned into the drive, I found myself gazing up past two floors of long bay windows to high balconies and tall chimney stacks that seemed able to touch the sky. The property was surrounded by gardens and in the distance there were glimpses of the sea. This was certainly a step up on anywhere we had lived before. (These days, it is a home for the elderly. A few years ago, Geoff and I visited an old friend there. I was amazed to find that she was living in 'my room'.)

We arrived at Hillbury late in the afternoon. Jean and I were told to go to the playroom, an enormous room with an open fire. Jean didn't hesitate. She dived into the toys. I don't think she had ever seen so many. I just stood in the dark hallway, feeling bewildered. I reached into my pocket and pulled out a note my father had given me. It was a short poem:

The day you went away
Words I could not say
My heart was very sad
Because you are leaving your dear old Dad.

Before we left, because I couldn't read and so I wouldn't forget, my father had repeated this to me several times. I guess it was his way of saying goodbye. Perhaps, deep down, despite hoping our stay would be short, he knew that we were not coming back?

Once Mr Hitchcock drove away, we found ourselves in the care of our two housemothers – Miss Phyllis Green and Miss Margaret Carr. 'Mageen', as we knew her, was in her late forties, the daughter of missionaries in Malaysia. She was motherly, but not one to give cuddles. Nevertheless, she loved to sing and played the piano well. She was also more than happy to read us stories. Being the eldest child in the house, I was allowed to stay up and had her attention and stories all to myself. As you can imagine, I loved that.

Miss Carr – 'Mo' – was in charge of the medical side of things. She was very different from Mageen. For a start, she appeared to have masses of money. She was a daughter of the Carr family in Carlisle, famous for their biscuits. It seemed that if there was anything new to be had, Mo went out and bought it. As I remember, she had a great liking for cameras and cars and contraptions. Intriguingly for the girls, she had a wardrobe of ball gowns and we were allowed to dress up in them. Needless to say, we got a lot of broken biscuits sent from the factory – sometimes we even got chocolate ones.

Mo was in her thirties, just a few weeks older than my mother. This I know, because when I was writing this book, I was able to contact her. She had just celebrated her hundredth birthday with a helicopter ride! I am glad to say she describes me as 'a gem' of a girl; full of fun, good at looking after the other children, and never known to tell on them when their games got out of hand.

*****

Hillbury was like an adventure playground; perfect if you wanted to play hide and seek. There were ten to twelve bedrooms, some big enough to take six beds. The kitchen was huge and the dining room not much smaller. I do remember there being acres of polished wooden floors, though this may be because I had a hand in polishing them. In the bathroom there was a Mabel Lucie Attwell picture, though I don't recall which of her rotund cherubs was charged with keeping an eye on the bathwater level.

Being the eldest child had some perks. I was blessed with my own room, whilst Jean had to share. There was a single bed, a desk for doing my homework, and a wardrobe for everything I possessed, which wasn't much. Our clothes were second-hand and I can't say I was always enamoured with them. We were never taken to the shops to choose our own. I was seventeen before I got to go into a shop and choose something new for myself. It is difficult to explain how daunting that was.

What I really loved was the garden. Hillbury was where my love of gardening started. Mageen enjoyed growing flowers, bringing bunches into the house, and there was a good fulltime gardener. We grew our own vegetables: peas, beans, carrots etc. In season I could pick apples and pears, raspberries, gooseberries and blackcurrants to my heart's content. When we had masses of fruit, I was taught how to bottle it and store it in the big pantry. I was given my own plot and packets of 'old-fashioned' flower seeds, like larkspur, to get me going. However, if the truth be known, I was more interested in the vegetable patch. This I put down to the fact that at Stanley growing food, not flowers, was more important to a hungry little girl.

There were seven girls and three boys permanently in the home, with others coming for brief stays or for holidays. We didn't get a holiday, but then we did have a beach on our doorstep. I am sure Mageen and Mo liked nothing better than to pack us off to the beach hut Hillbury owned, from where we could swim and play to our heart's content all day long. When we were older, in the spring and autumn, the ten of us were given sandwiches, sausages and a frying pan. Then we were driven or rode our bicycles out to the fields around Greenaleigh Farm or further west to the old look-out station at Hurlstone Point. We built a fire, cooked 'Cheese Dreams' – open, toasted, cheese sandwiches – and the sausages, and skipped pebbles across the sea. Whenever the 'orphans' from Bristol visited, it was a great opportunity for a mass picnic. Around ninety sandwiches, plus a piece of cake for everyone, had to be made and stacked neatly into tins.

Needless to say, Hillbury wasn't all play and picnics. We all had jobs to do. On Saturdays I had to polish the dining room floor; first by hand and then with a special machine to buff up the wood. It took me all morning to get from one end to the other and back again. When we had visitors, I was in often in charge of peeling potatoes. The house had a gadget to help with this, perhaps one of Mo's many purchases. I had to place all the potatoes in the contraption and turn the tap on to wash them. Then I had to wind the handle until the spikes in the machine took off all the peel. Whatever the merits of the machine, it took a lot of winding I can tell you! Jean's job was to do the dusting. I still remember her doing the bathrooms shelves. She had a very efficient technique. She would climb onto a stool, 'whoosh' all the brushes and combs off the shelf, wipe it well, and then spend several minutes neatly putting everything back.

*****

As you can tell, I was very happy at Hillbury. I had the stability of being in one place for years, not months. As the eldest child I enjoyed the responsibilities Mageen and Mo gave me and became more confident. I had six sisters (and three brothers) to play with – whether we were camped in the Hillbury beach hut, clattering around the house with our games, digging in the garden, or sitting in our favourite tree on North Hill. Life, at last, could just be fun. Most importantly, I now had two 'mothers'; both of whom cared for me, and who, I knew, were never going to send me away.

Our father visited, taking us out for tea two or three times a year, but this was always a little awkward. Most of the other children didn't get visits and Jean and I were asked not to talk about our time with him. On one occasion, my

Dad brought a bicycle for us. We were very embarrassed. Mageen and Mo had to go out and buy cycles for all the other children. I think the point is that we were a real family at Hillbury. It was great having other children and people visit, but in truth we liked it best when it was just us.

Chapter 12

Decisions, Decisions

Like most children of the 1950s, two things dominated my life. School and church. Only Saturday was a day off, although at Hillbury, as I have said, there was more than enough to keep me busy. As it happened, Jean and I arrived at Easter, so there was plenty of church to fill the first few days. Then, all too soon, the holidays were gone and I started at yet another new school, Minehead Junior.

Right from the beginning Mageen and Mo made sure I knew my role as 'biggest sister'. Each morning I had to get up around seven and wake the other children. Over the years I did pretty well with my duties, but one winter day I messed up big time. I woke up and looked at the clock. It was ten past seven. Ten minutes late! I hurried out of bed and headed for the other rooms, waking the children, and hastily getting them dressed. I should not have been so hassled. Mageen stumbled sleepily in, asking what was going on. It was twenty-five to two. I had to put all the children back to bed again. It was no wonder they were very grumpy.

On weekdays, once we were all decent, we clattered as quietly as we could manage down the stairs. Breakfast with Mageen and Mo was porridge or cereal, with toast. Then we were sent off to school, me shepherding my troop of tinies up the hill to the infant school, a ten-minute walk away. I left them at the school gates and made my own way to the juniors across the road. At the end of my day the others were already home, so I had to walk back to Hillbury by myself.

Supper – essentially 'high tea', because we had eaten a proper lunch at school – came with rules. There was bread and a choice. You either had bread and butter, or bread and jam. Taking butter *and* jam was not allowed. And if you had jam, you weren't allowed sugar in your tea. On special occasions, bless our cook, we were treated with cake.

I remember my father once brought us a big slab of butter. This disappeared into the 'adult's pantry'. Each evening Mageen and Mo would sit in front of the fire, toasting bread and enjoying 'our' butter. The scrumptious smell wafting up to our rooms was both heavenly and agony. (They also regularly ate chocolate biscuits, which was another sore point!) So, one day I crept down to the big pantry and found the butter on the shelf. Carefully, I cut off a good-sized slither and smothered a small cracker with it. Feeling very pleased with myself, I sat and ate it, savouring it to the last crumb. Afterwards, somehow, I felt justice had been done.

Before cocoa and bed, we were allowed to play or read. I often used the time to feed and clean out my rabbit, which we kept in the conservatory. He was another orphan for Hillbury's collection. I had seen him in the garden; a quivering bundle of wild grey fur, small enough to sit on the palm of my hand. When he was still there twenty-four hours later, I was allowed to keep him. We fed him for a while with a medicine dropper and he survived his ordeal. In fact, he lived in the house for ten years, outlasting my stay.

Minehead Junior School proved a good move. I was thankful to have a good headmistress, who spotted that I needed help. Slowly, I got to see words instead of meaningless jumbles of letters on the pages of books. Numbers and sums started to make sense. It was progress, of a sort, even if I was way behind.

The biggest blessing was that I found myself a husband. Or perhaps he found me? Geoff was already in the class. In many ways there was little to connect us, apart from the fact that this was a small school and it was difficult to avoid each other. Geoff was an only child, very shy, the son of the manager of a local department store. I had a family of nine noisy siblings and was well able to make my presence felt. He lived in a stable family home, in a very upmarket (as far as I was concerned) semi-detached looking out on North Hill. Effectively, I was an orphan in an institution. He was one of the brighter ones. I certainly was not.

Mageen and Mo encouraged us to invite friends to the house. Strangely, they were never allowed to play, only to have tea. For some reason – perhaps because of who we were – we seemed, for want of better words, to be always picking up 'waifs and strays'. There were a couple of children who used to visit regularly. Their mother ran a shop and didn't have a lot of time for them. I guess one of the boys at Hillbury invited Geoff because he was a little lonely. I didn't pay him much attention, it has to be said. That came later.

At the end of the term Geoff and I moved on to a secondary modern school in Watery Lane, just down the hill from the junior school. Sorry to disappoint you, but there was no school romance. No offers to carry my bag. No dawdling in the corridors before class. A couple of years later, Geoff did well and transferred to the grammar school. After that, our main contact was through church. As far as I was concerned, he was 'just a boy', although apparently I was beginning to make an impression on him.

The secondary modern was the first school that I really loved. I made some good friends there. Wearing a school uniform meant less worry about my second-hand clothes. Academically, there were no great expectations for the pupils, which suited me. Even if I didn't learn a great deal, there was a lot to keep me entertained and build my confidence. Gym lessons were always good. I won the hundred yards dash on Sports Day. I particularly liked home economics and cookery, which complemented my attempts at baking at Hillbury. Maths always remained a mystery, but I did enjoy English. Encouraged by the headmistress, I discovered a love of poetry and used to learn poems for fun. The fact that I was top of the class in the subject boosted my self-esteem no end. I was poor at languages, but learned to count in both French and German very competently. One of our teachers allocated us numbers and each morning we had to call out our number at registration; one morning in English, the next in French, and the following day in German. Unfortunately, we never did learn to count beyond thirty.

All the pupils left the secondary modern at fifteen with no qualifications at all. Anyone with any prospects was at the grammar school. Most went into farming or got jobs in shops and the local cafes. Mind you, some did better than others. I remember the school had a special 'Five Boys' class for a group of farmers' sons, who could neither read nor write. One of them became a millionaire, having started out selling veg and fruit off a barrow. Such were my anticipated prospects that I wasn't even entered for any exams. I did go to night classes to try and get an English O-level, but after I failed twice, they said I wouldn't be entered again. A-levels were never discussed!

One thing I was good at was organising children – perhaps something to do with living at Hillbury, where I got a lot of practice. In my final year, I became Head Girl. No small honour but masses of responsibility. I had to keep the lower classes in line on the way to and from our lunch at the Women's Institute down the road. When it rained, I had to supervise the pupils in the hall during the breaks. By the time I finished school, I wasn't the bewildered little girl who had arrived in Minehead trying to make sense of what was happening to me. I was a much more confident individual. I left knowing that I could and would achieve things in life.

*****

God was the other constant in my life as I grew up. Hillbury, being a Christian charity, had a strict duty to keep us on the straight and narrow. Every morning at breakfast we had prayers and a Bible reading. Grace was said at every meal. Sundays were special, which was good but not-so-good. The main not-so-good was that we were not allowed to play games. We could only read, which wasn't that great for me. Nevertheless, Sunday was 'meat day'. On Saturdays we only had soup and mashed potato, but on Sunday a joint was put in the Aga and I made two sponge puddings – usually syrup or spotted dick, putting them on to boil. We were perhaps keener to get out of church than our elders felt we should be.

On rainy days we went to church in Mo's car. These were the days when a lot of liberties were taken with safety. It doesn't take much working out that getting ten children and two adults into a car was an art in itself. Mo drove, of course. One child sat in the front on Mageen's knee and there were eight squeezed in the back. Which left me. My 'seat' was in the boot. Can you imagine the consternation there would be today if you turned up at church, popped open the boot, and a child tumbled out? I did just that for years.

When it wasn't raining, we had to walk. By some peculiar adult reasoning we could travel by car, but cycling was forbidden. With a morning service and Sunday School in the afternoon, that was four miles walked in a day for the little ones. Some weeks we had to go three times.

From my seat in the chapel the morning services were nothing but a bore from start to finish. This was a Plymouth Brethren Church – and it was grim! The brethren were very few, very devout, and their services seemingly carved on tablets of stone, as unchangeable as the Ten Commandments. With no pastor to guide the proceedings, every Sunday the same people stood up and said much the same things. One old man intoned week in, week out, 'Lord, anoint our eyes with eye salve'; a reference to Jesus' words to a not-so-hot church in what is now Turkey. (I am sure the man considered his Minehead congregation far from 'wretched, pitiful, poor, blind and naked', as the Laodiceans are described in the book of Revelation.) I'm afraid I used to mimic him terribly.

Nevertheless, as I entered my teens, I was exploring the claims of Christianity and beginning to find a home there as well. I had always believed in God, always prayed – 'everyone' did. My mother's Russian Orthodoxy had little influence in our family life, but the army was built around being British and, therefore, 'Christian'. Even in the miseries of Stanley, God was not forgotten. There were more than twenty denominations represented by clergy, missionaries and congregations. Come what may we met on Sundays and on special holy days.

My father had a nominal faith in his youth and the early years of his marriage. His declared denomination was Baptist, although on another army form he describes himself as belonging to the Plymouth Brethren. At the time I am not sure if he was aware of the difference. However, in his thirties, he came into contact with people like Mr Hitchcock and it did make a real impact on his life. He gave up alcohol and his Christian faith became plain in his work ethic, something openly noted by his superiors. In 1954, when the American evangelist, Billy Graham, visited London, my father went along and at one of the meetings at Harringay 'went forward', as they say. I do believe this was when he fully committed himself to following Jesus.

My Dad had some spiritual influence on me, but it was mainly others who helped me along the way. My carers – the Heap family, the Pearsons, Mageen and Mo – were all Christians, keen for me to be at church, read my Bible, and pray. I remember that one of the Heap daughters asked me to give my life to Jesus. Eager to please, I said yes but with little understanding. However, in my teens, things were different. I was learning a lot and it was becoming personal. It became clear that a response was needed. Was I willing to follow Jesus? Was I going let God have a say in my life? Yes..? Or no?

I joined a Sunday evening youth group which met in the home of one of my school teachers. The meeting was run by our church and the church Geoff went to, Millbridge

Evangelical Free Church, where his father was a church leader. The number of young people was quite small in both churches, so it made sense to meet together. Inevitably, it was a great place to begin to build relationships. Geoff's interest in me was becoming obvious. To him at least. Me? I still didn't have a clue.

Minehead was a good venue for Christian summer camps. Each year a large sand 'pulpit' was built on the beach near the seawall and we had a week of children's activities; lots of games, with some serious moments when someone would speak, hymns were sung, prayers were said. A man we knew as 'Uncle Tom' brought along his squeezebox and played it for the songs. Geoff has a very clear memory of me standing up on the pulpit and singing:

Living he loved me, dying he saved me,

Buried, He carried my sins far away

Rising, He justified freely forever

One day He's coming

Oh, glorious day.

Funnily enough, I remember looking out over the heads of the children and seeing him too. I don't think our eyes met across a crowded beach, but perhaps something was stirring in me after all. Nevertheless, Geoff's request for a date, when it finally arrived, was just embarrassing!

I had a friend called Elizabeth and she *was* keen on Geoff.

'Can you ask him to go out with me?'

'Why don't you?'

'I can't... please.'

I agreed and trotted off to find Geoff.

'Geoff?'

'Yes…'

'Elizabeth would like to go out with you.'

'Er… No…' There was a pause, a deep breath, a rush. 'But I'll take you out.'

Oops. That wasn't supposed to happen. What on earth was I supposed to tell Elizabeth?

More to the point what was I to say to Geoff. Yes... or no?

But I digress! There was another important decision to be made.

I went to the church and asked to be baptised. I was fifteen and I was making a public statement that, as the song said, Jesus loved me and had died on the cross for me. From then on, I would be letting God guide my life, although I hadn't the remotest notion just where in the world he was planning on taking me. As it happened, the next stop was no further than Taunton and I would get to ride on the footplate of the engine taking the train from Minehead.

Chapter 13

Nissen Nursing

I said 'yes' to Geoff. And then I had to go and talk to Elizabeth. She was not happy. Fortunately, she forgave me for ruining her dreams of a boyfriend and we remained friends for many years afterwards until her death from cancer. She too became a missionary. She studied at the same Bible college as Geoff. Unhappily, she had a broken engagement with another student, and then went out to Ivory Coast as a teacher and church worker.

As for me and my first – but not only – boyfriend, everything went well for a while. We enjoyed our 'dates'. Looking back, it is difficult to explain just how innocent we were. There were bike rides out into West Somerset or walks on Exmoor. Plenty of church activities. I don't think we ever went to the cinema.

We had, of course, both been raised on stern-faced Christian morality. Mageen trusted us to behave ourselves! Plus, Geoff was as shy as a shadow on a cloudy day. When, eventually, my father met him, Geoff hardly said a word. My Dad took me on one side and offered his advice, 'Put him back where you found him'. I didn't, but all the same, at the end of our schooling, we were heading in different directions. Geoff had the opportunity to do A-levels and perhaps to go to college. I had very definite plans of my own. It was all a bit traditional for a girl, but I really wanted to become a nurse.

My decision to go into nursing developed while I was at Minehead Secondary Modern. Perhaps my Dad being an orderly was part of it, but my love of nursing really blossomed when I joined St John Ambulance. I liked the uniform; crisp, grey, short-sleeved dresses with white collars and cuffs, and neat white headscarves tied at the back of our heads. So, I enrolled and discovered I was good at First Aid. I really liked being confronted with emergency situations. Plus, there were badges and certificates to be earned and we travelled up and down the country to competitions. Our team often did well, winning cups and prizes.

Back home, Mageen, as well as caring for us, was looking after her mother. Granny Green was rarely well. Feeling very pleased with myself, I used to put on my uniform and trot down to her room to help care for her. I made her bed, gave her bed baths, and generally was at her beck and call. She could be very demanding and was happy to take advantage of this willing young 'nurse'. Nevertheless, I didn't mind. I was enjoying myself.

There was, in part, also a pragmatic reason behind all this. At seventeen I would have to leave Hillbury and I had no family home to return to. Nursing would provide accommodation. Otherwise what was I to do, where would I live?

It goes without saying that in the 1950s, as now, you couldn't become a nurse without qualifications. Minehead Secondary Modern was never going to help me there. So, I needed to pass some exams to even contemplate nursing as a profession. The answer to this was to enrol at what we called Taunton Tech. It was an hour or so away on the train, but there were few other options open to me.

So, in September 1956, I walked down to the railway station on the Minehead seafront, boarded the steam train to Taunton, and made my way to the technical college; my first day of a two-year course. I was only fifteen, but I don't remember being particularly concerned about travelling alone. I had changed into quite a happy extrovert with a positive outlook on life. I was eager to engage with whoever was going my way. I guess that is how I got to know the train driver.

Trains to Taunton and beyond started at Minehead, so things were more relaxed than at the stations en route. There was no rush for passengers to get aboard, the engine spouting steam, and the guard's whistle demanding the carriage doors be slammed shut. I really disliked being late, just as I had done as a child, so was usually on the platform well in time for my journey. While we waited for the signal to leave, the train driver was, I discovered, equally glad of a chat. One day he asked me if I wanted to hop up onto the engine footplate. Whether this was allowed I had no idea, but the opportunity was too good to miss. He and the fireman did all the hard work. I sounded the whistle when told to. We chugged down the track quite a way, through Dunster and Blue Anchor, before he told me I'd better get into one of the carriages. I am sure he was worried about his job as we got closer to Taunton.

I did well at the Tech. I got a couple of 'O'-levels – geography and economics. More importantly, I did my pre-nursing course. It wasn't easy getting my head around all the new medical terms that came my way. Reading wasn't too bad, but trying to write answers to homework and exam questions was a nightmare. In the end I gave myself lines. Evening after evening I retreated to my room and painstakingly copied out one hundred times the phrases and words that I needed to learn. Thankfully, this laborious process did work and I passed my Prelim Part 1. Another good thing was that I made a new friend; a girl called Sylvia, who was a Christian. She got on the same train as me at a village called Williton, about half way to our destination. We always sat together in class and, as I will explain, I probably have to thank her and her father for getting me a place at Bristol Royal Infirmary (BRI).

After Taunton Tech I was confronted with a number of quandaries. I had basic qualifications, but nowhere near enough to get into general nursing training at BRI, where competition for places was fierce. Plus, even if my qualifications had been adequate, I was still too young to apply. And thirdly, I now had nowhere to live. I decided to enrol on a course in orthopaedic nursing at Winford Hospital, south of Bristol. This would give me accommodation. Also, when – if – I passed, I would have another nursing certificate to hopefully push me up the ladder a little.

Winford was a next to nothing village and the hospital was about a mile away, out in the sticks. It was a sprawling site, pocketed with Nissen huts, surrounded by countryside. Walking from one ward to the next could take five minutes. The huts were designed so that one wall would open onto lawns. This meant we could push the TB patients out into the fresh air. There was more than one occasion when we had to shoo cows that had escaped from a nearby field out of the wards. In the winter we were given small capes to wear, so that we could make up the beds in the snow!

The best ward was the male ward, where most of the 'boys' had suffered motorbike accidents. They were a cheerful lot generally and teased us without mercy. The most distressing ward was the children with congenital deformities. Their parents were only able to visit twice a week – Wednesdays and Sundays. You can imagine how harrowing it was to have to quieten rows of distraught children when their parents left.

The worst ward was the one for female femur patients. They were hard work. Thirty women all needing bedpans. Ward rules said patients had to be washed and 'panned' before eight a.m. When I was on my own (usually there were two on the ward, with one acting as the 'runner' between wards), I started waking the women up at four, bathing a few at a time and then letting them sleep again, so that I could meet the deadline. All the pans had to be hand-washed with disinfectant, dried, and put out on the trolley for the morning shift. It could be a living nightmare if there was a demand for pans all through the early hours.

It was by no means easy, but I soon began to thrive at Winford. We worked hard. Day shifts and night shifts, lectures each morning, private study in our own time. This was real nursing and I soaked up as much knowledge as I could. I noted down everything I felt was useful and memorised it. When it came to the exams, I wrote something on everything on the grounds that I was sure to get a few marks for each question. My method obviously worked. I never failed an exam there.

Working at Winford also meant I was paid while studying. Student nurses got ten pounds a month after board, lodging and tax. Having serious money of my own was a huge change for me. At Hillbury we had been given pocket money. Two pence per week. It was expected that we would put one penny in the church collection. I was astute enough to know that this amounted to half my income and that the church preached only tithing a tenth. What to do? I changed my money into farthings and dutifully dropped one farthing into the bag each week. I was always very proud when the collection was announced. So many pounds, so many shillings, so many pennies and *one farthing*. That was my farthing.

To my shame one of the first things I needed to do with my salary at Winford was buy some new clothes. Not just because I wanted things of my own, rather than hand-me-downs. The real problem was that I was eating too well. The food in the canteen was free. I had never seen such portions in my life. I began eating like Oliver – more was always on the menu. I could eat fish and chips with macaroni cheese and two puddings in one sitting. I arrived at Winford weighing seven and a half stone. A few months later I was pushing eleven. Only when I saw a photo of myself did I get to grips with my new fat self and regulate my diet with a harsh decree of self-control.

Nevertheless, I was now in desperate need of clothes that fitted me. I caught a bus to Bristol and ventured into a shop. I had no idea what to do! Eventually, I found a bra I liked, and was so embarrassed that I paid for it and ran. One bra only goes so far in the weekly wash. A week later I had to go back to buy another. I remember that around the same time I bought a pair of trousers. Very risqué in 1958.

The time at Winford was great, but I was eager to get to BRI. The trouble was that I was not guaranteed a place, even with my Prelim Part 1 and orthopaedic certificate. I needed to have an interview and to do an exam. The interview I could cope with. The exam was an intelligence test. I liked to think I was intelligent, but I am not sure I wanted my claim to be tested.

Remarkably, when I sat down and looked at the exam paper, I realised that I already knew the answers to the questions. Sometime before I had been to stay with Sylvia, who, being older, had gone to BRI before me. Her father was doing some puzzles. Sylvia said they were the kind of thing she had been asked to do to get into BRI. I watched as she and her father worked them out. Now I was looking at the same puzzles. It is possibly the only exam I have ever smiled my way through. Needless to say, I passed. With my orthopaedic certificate I enrolled for the final two years of the normal three-year course.

As far as I was concerned this was all going very well. I was having a lot of fun, despite the hard work. However, God was not getting much of a look-in. Having left the nurture of Hillbury, I struggled. I rarely went to church. Shifts made it hard to make it to services. I found little interest in Christianity among the majority of my colleagues. The only time I got any encouragement in my faith was when I did a three-month course at Bristol and a staff nurse helped another student and me start a Christian Union.

Meanwhile, Geoff was doing very well. At seventeen, he finished at the grammar school and got a job up in London; living at the Young Men's Christian Association in Fulham. He was working for the Civil Service – a clerk in the Aerodrome Fire Service of the Ministry of Civil Aviation. From what I could gather he was buying firefighting equipment and making sure the men maintained it. He had plans to go to Bible college, once he had some money in hand.

Now we were apart he sent me letters. Long letters. Mainly about his Christian life. They were very earnest, very spiritual. Not exactly what a girl was hoping for! Inevitably, we began to drift apart. We still wrote from time to time but just as friends. What was more pressing were my father's affairs. About a year before I went to Winford, he had announced he wanted to annul his marriage to my mother. And then he told Jean and me that he was getting married.

Chapter 14

Family Affairs

The ulcer that put my Dad in hospital when Jean and I went to Hillbury brought his army career to an end. He was on a milk drip for weeks, months even, and clearly no longer able to do his job. It must have been dreadful to lie there day after day worrying about his wife and his children, unable to do anything to help us. In March 1952 – almost a year to the day Mr Hitchcock had taken us into care – my father was asked to sign the official secrets act; a formality, I assume. Two days later he was on 'invaliding leave' for four weeks. Then, 'terminal leave' for another four and that was that. His army life was over.

It was a sad end to seventeen years of military service. Like so many other things, he never spoke about it to me, but I am sure it must have seemed yet another misfortune in a procession of troubles that had blighted his desire for a normal family life. If there was any good to come out of it, he certainly did significantly better than his Uncle John. He got a wonderful recommendation:

> Military conduct: Exemplary.
> Testimonies: This NCO is known to be a diligent worker, conscientious and thoroughly trustworthy. He is a total abstainer and by his own example a Christian leader.
> Recommended for employment.

It helps me to know that, through all his troubles, he maintained an excellent reputation and that he had a practical faith, leading his men by example. Nevertheless, at thirty-eight and in depressed post-war Britain, he was walking the streets, looking for work. Whether it was just a job that came up or my Dad had contacts in the dockyards at Southampton, I do not know. One way or another he ended up making a very significant career change; working as a steward on cruise liners.

For a while he was on ships sailing to Sydney, which gave him an opportunity to contact my grandmother, Eugenia, and my uncle, Leo. Leo had done well for himself. He was working as a manager in a record manufacturing business and living in the suburbs of Sydney – at the foot of the Blue Mountains, on a very pleasant wide boulevard of bungalows, with his wife, Nadia. She, you will remember, was the wife of William Seraphina at Stanley Camp. At the end of the war the family had sailed to Australia and the plan was for them to return to Britain. William went to Scotland with his son, Billy, and daughter, Vera. Nadia and two of their children, Elizabeth and Margaret, did not go with them. According to the *Dundee Courier* Nadia had beri-beri, but I do wonder if that was William's story to ease his embarrassment over his domestic affairs. By the time the family arrived in Australia, the marriage was apparently finished. Leo had usurped Nadia's affections. Eventually, Billy and Vera joined their mother. Leo had an instant family, as well as he and Nadia having a son of their own, Robert.

This is something of a strange story, as Leo and Nadia did not marry in a civil ceremony until 1953. What happened over the eight years after the war and why they would wait is not clear. Perhaps divorce at a distance was not an easy affair. They were living in the same suburb, on the same street – perhaps, scandalously, in the same house? More mysterious is the fact that Leo had adopted a new name by deed poll, Sterling – presumably to make it easier to get work – but continued to use Borisoff on electoral forms, even when married to 'Nadia Sterling'. Perhaps most puzzling is how my father ever found them at all.

My grandmother had kept her surname, but now liked to be known as Jenny. She was also in Sydney. Anatol had died, so she would have been on her own, living near to the waterfront on Botany Bay with her greyhounds. This was another very spacious suburb, the roads lined with trees and neat grass verges, which must have made my father envious in his own beleaguered circumstances. Kindly, she sent me a copy of *The Jungle Book*, inscribed with a greeting and her name. I kept it for many years, but in one of our moves it was lost; something I do regret. Leo died in 1984 and had his ashes spread on Brisbane Water, north of Sydney. When Eugenia died and where she is buried, I haven't been able to find out. Surprisingly, she apparently wasn't interred with her husband.

To be honest, Jean and I learned too little from my father's visit to Australia. He didn't think to tell us and we were not curious enough to ask. We were possibly more interested in the presents he brought back – for me, a toy koala bear, which may be expected, and a Japanese silk kimono, which would not. After that contact with my Australian relatives was lost for sixty years, until through the writing of this book Robert and I found each other online and began to swap our family histories.

What was quite wonderful was that in Robert's old family photo albums were three black and white photos of people he did not recognise – a woman in a thick coat with two cute children, and then two other photos of the children alone. The children, of course, are Jean and I; the woman, our mother. One of them is clearly taken on the lawn at Hillbury. I can only think that these were photographs – which I had never seen until now – that my Dad took to Sydney with him and left with Eugenia and Leo.

My Dad's next move was to transfer to Cunard shipping and work on ships to the States. It was here he met a nurse and midwife, Gladys Roe. She was divorced and liked to be called 'Steve' or 'Stevie', a throwback to her maiden name, Stephens. Remarkably, my mother and her shared their birthdays, though Stevie was a couple of years older. She was a ship's officer, whereas my father was a steward. The company rule was that never the twain should meet. Obviously, they contravened that particular rule out on the Atlantic quite successfully.

To be frank, I think it was a marriage of convenience. They were two lonely people with a shared interest in nursing, filling spare time on a tedious sea trip, but with little more in common. She had no children of her own and was not a Christian. After the wedding in Liverpool in April 1958, she lived in Southampton, while my father continued to work for Cunard. Consequently, he was away as much as he was with her, which did little to maintain their relationship.

There was, of course, the dilemma of my Mum. She was in no condition to recognise my Dad, let alone understand that they were married. I believe that he had the marriage annulled, no doubt citing my Mum's mental health. This leaves me in a strange place. In effect it means that my parents' marriage was never valid. Legally, I am the daughter of a marriage that never existed. At the time this was not my quandary. I just hoped my father would be happy, though that was never really the case.

*****

As Britain steadied itself to embrace the Swinging Sixties, my immediate concerns were with my nurse training at Bristol. At first, I found being in a city quite daunting. I was lonely and at a loss to know what to do with my days off. I wasn't welcome in Southampton, unless my father was home. On occasions I was able to cadge a lift to Hillbury for a weekend, sleeping in my old room, which was delightful. In the hospital I was a bit lost too. Suddenly, I was one of a large group of nurses, not enjoying the fun of working with a small group of friends. My confidence floundered. I became nervous around my colleagues and the senior staff.

Like Britain and the Sixties, it took me a while to get into the swing of things.

Moving to Bristol in September 1960 was positive on two accounts. The work on the wards and the high standards of teaching were brilliant as far as I was concerned. It also gave me the opportunity to get to church and rebuild my faith. My first thought was to find George Muller's church in the city. However, his original chapel, Bethesda, had been bombed in the Second World War, so I settled at the 'Clifton Bethesda', a daughter church about a half hour's walk from the hospital. It was here that the minister encouraged us to write regularly to a missionary. I was paired with a nurse in a leprosy hospital in India. Little did I think when I wrote her my first letter that some years later I would be in India, working in a leprosy hospital too.

I won't give you a day by day account of my time at Bristol, except to tell you a story about finding accommodation at the end of my first year. Sylvia, another Christian nurse called Bunty, and I found a flat a bus ride from the hospital. The place was freezing with next to no bedding provided, but we managed to scrape enough together to make it quite homely.

One Sunday at church, I got talking to a good-looking young man – a sailor studying for his sailing exams – or was he talking to me? I invited Peter back to the flat for coffee. He told us his landlady was being a real pain. She wouldn't let him do his laundry in the house. We girls were ever so sympathetic and offered him a key to our flat. He could do his smalls when we were at work, hang them out on the line, and have them out of sight by the time we returned. What we had not foreseen was that the couple upstairs had a keen eye for scandal. They complained to the landlord that we were living in sin. He threw us out without asking for an explanation. My first – and only – eviction!

At the end of the course we did our exams and on the appropriate day all filed down to the post office to collect our results. BRI had a tradition. The PO workers would keep the envelopes, handing them out to the nurses individually. So, at five in the morning we tumbled nervously out on to the dark silent streets. Tradition also had it that you waited until everyone had arrived before you were allowed to open your envelope. The tension was palpable by the time everyone had assembled, I can tell you.

I had passed. That, as I will tell you, wasn't a surprise. What is more I had been awarded the hospital's silver medal, the second best student in my year. Now, that was a shock. I would get a certificate and ten pounds, no small sum, which I spent on a camera. I was ecstatic. I had come a long way from leaving Minehead Secondary Modern with no qualifications, other than a bundle of enthusiasm for becoming a nurse.

Apart from a couple of students who had not passed, we trooped back en masse to the hospital, had breakfast, and then lined up to collect our pink staff nurse uniforms. Everyone told me the colour suited me. In truth, I think my face must have been glowing with delight and matched the pink perfectly.

There were two reasons I went to the post office feeling confident. Perversely, in my final year I had suffered terribly with sore throats. I ended up in my own hospital having my tonsils out and being nursed by my colleagues. I was a week in bed and then went down to Hillbury to recuperate. Mageen's niece, Mo's replacement, collected me in the car. (Mo had possibly left because she and Mageen's mother never got on. Granny Green was forever ordering people about and Miss Carr of Carr's biscuits was not from a family prepared to put up with that.) For three weeks I lounged in the warmth of the sun outside the conservatory, poring over my notes, drawing detailed diagrams of every organ from the head to the abdomen and below, and writing volumes on muscles, meds and ward management. By the time I was back in Bristol I had a great tan and I was well prepared for my final exams.

If the written papers went well, my oral went like a dream. On the ward I had nursed a woman with cancer. The treatment – a first in our hospital – had been to remove her pituitary gland down through her nose. I was her nurse before and after the operation and her theatre nurse as well. My examiner had never seen a case like this. I was full of information – details of the surgery, what drugs were needed, how she had been cared for pre and post-op. My examiner was clearly impressed. I walked out of her office confident that I had passed, determined not to breathe a word of it to anyone else.

I stayed in Bristol as a staff nurse for another year, but then it was time to move on again. I applied for and got a place on a midwifery course at Mile End Hospital in Stepney. I needed to be in London. It was time for Geoff and I to get to know each other a lot better.

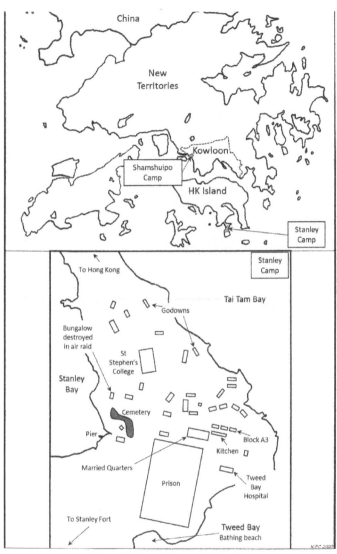

Map of Hong Kong & Stanley

Parents wedding day 1940

With mother Elizabeth 1941

At 'Hillbury', Minehead

Queen Mary Ward, Bristol Royal Infirmary, 1962

Father Alfred on board the 'Queen Mary'

Presentation of Silver Medal, B.R.I., 1962

Wedding to Geoff 1964

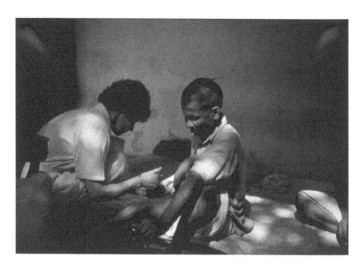

Treating patient, Muzaffarpur Leprosy Hospital, 1967

Family on motorbike 1970

Geoff, Mark & Rachel 1970

Scottish holiday 1988

In Tibetan part of China 1990

Godmanchester 2009

Golden Wedding 2014

Chapter 15

All About Trains?

It is strange how trains – Geoff being something of an enthusiast for all things railways – have played a small but significant part in my story. My renewed relationship with Geoff came about because I caught a train he missed.

As I have mentioned, after he had gone off to work in London and I headed for Winford and Bristol, Geoff and I wrote to each other. Well, to be honest, he wrote to me and generally I didn't write back, except once in a while. We were friends but no more than that. In fact, I went out with Peter, my church-going student sailor, for a time, but that never got serious.

Then, at Christmas 1962, just after my registration as a qualified nurse, both Geoff and I were in Minehead, where we met up at a friend's house.

'Can I see you off from the station in the morning?' Geoff asked as we left.

This was totally unnecessary. I knew my way around the Minehead-Bristol line miles better than him. But... nice of him, I thought. Suddenly, I was back where I had been about six years before.

Yes… or no?

'Yes,' I hesitated. 'Yes, of course.'

Come the time for the train to depart, I was there on my lonesome. Not exactly being stood up – this was hardly a date – but, all the same, I was aggrieved he had not turned up.

A couple of days later I received another of Geoff's letters. An apology. And a note to say he was still on vacation from London Bible College (now London School of Theology), where he was studying for a degree. He could come up to Bristol. Would that be OK? This time he got a decisive reply – yes.

There was bad snow that New Year. Geoff arrived in less than debonair wellington boots. However, neither footwear nor weather could spoil the day. We were oblivious to the cold as we chatted away like the good friends we were. Something deeper warmed us. Thereafter, letter-writing was no longer avoided and now and again we stretched to a few pence in a public phone box to talk.

One of the things that brought us closer was India. Geoff, I discovered, had been regularly going to a prayer meeting to pray for the country. His enthusiasm matched mine. He wanted to go to India as a missionary. I had the same idea. God, it seemed, was saying something. Friendship quickly turned to love. By March, less than three months later, we were engaged.

Our engagement was a bit of an odd event. We travelled to my Dad's small semi-detached bungalow in Bitterne, Southampton, to tell him and Stevie our news and then went downtown to buy a ring. I was keen to get a ruby with the obligatory diamonds. But where were we to get engaged? Neither of us were particularly familiar with the city. We trailed around the streets for a while, until Geoff spotted a greying stucco Victorian church which was badly in need of a coat of paint. The doors were ajar. We slipped into this ageing barn of an auditorium and sat beneath the balcony on a hard pew, praying no-one would disturb us. Geoff asked the important question. I said 'yes' yet again. Then we walked back out onto the streets of Southampton. Not very romantic, but we were happy. I was less happy with the shop that sold us the ring. When I had it repaired several years later, the jeweller informed me that the ruby wasn't a ruby at all!

Engagement, inevitably, led to me applying for the midwifery course in London. Now Geoff and I could see each other more often. When I arrived at Mile End, I was informed that the hospital was a 'signs and wonders' hospital. There was a big influx of Greek and Turkish Cypriots into our area. Few, if any, of the pregnant women spoke English. Husbands wouldn't venture onto the wards during delivery, so their children were brought in to explain to their mothers what the midwives wanted them to do. Christians on staff, familiar with the Bible's references to 'signs and wonders', jokingly applied the phrase to their work. The midwives made the signs and the women wondered at them.

My time there ended abruptly halfway through the course. I got a letter from Mageen. She had retired from Hillbury and bought a house with her widowed sister. Now, the sister was dying from cancer. Mageen was not coping. Would I consider helping her out? It was difficult to refuse my housemother. The downside was that Mageen did not pay me for my services. I was forced to get an afternoon job at the seafront gift store run by my future father-in-law. There was one advantage, however. Geoff and I had planned our wedding at his church in Minehead for that August. Being in the town would help me prepare.

A few days before the wedding I was serving in the shop when a couple came in and introduced themselves. They were the Heaps – my carers from way back in chapter two – down from Liverpool, on holiday. My expression must have been priceless. I have no idea how they knew where to find me or that I was getting married. I had been eight the last time I had seen them. I had lived the majority of my life wondering why they didn't want me and now here they were, as nice as new neighbours, asking about the wedding. It was quite surreal. We weren't able to invite them to the service, but it was kind of them to come and find me.

The 22 August 1964 was as sunny as they come. There was an abundance of clergy in attendance. We were married by Geoff's uncle, a former pastor at the church, with the present Millbridge minister helping out. Another minister, Stuart, was the best man. Geoff – a prospective pastor – was nicely turned out in a black suit, with a silver tie, a well-pressed handkerchief in his breast pocket and the extravagance of *two* white carnations in his lapel.

I had been back to Southampton to buy my dress. My father had generously offered fifty pounds to pay for it and the reception at a local hotel, to which we had invited about fifty guests. As always, I was clear what I wanted. A modest, uncluttered, heavy satin dress with long sleeves, tied at the waist. (No train though!) Just twenty pounds – a price that pleased my stepmother. The shoes and my veil I bought myself.

For the bridesmaids' dresses we went upmarket. Harrods in London had offcuts of jacquard silk. I managed to find enough material for a dress for Jean and for Sue, a nursing friend at Bristol and Mile End – Jean in apple green, Sue in vibrant blue. I had a white satin rose on my veil and a dozen pink roses in my white heather bouquet. When the dresses were finished, there was enough material to have roses made for the bridesmaids' hair. Jean and Sue got good wear out of those dresses. After the wedding, by mistake, Geoff and I drove away in his father's car with the bridesmaids' 'ordinary' clothes on the back seat. They had to make their way home on the train in all their finery.

*****

We had our honeymoon in Salcombe in Devon and then headed back to north-east London. Geoff was about to become the pastor's assistant at an evangelical church in South Woodford. This was, however, simply a stepping stone to going to India with an organisation called Regions Beyond Missionary Union (RBMU), which I will tell you more about in the next chapter. Believe it or not, a train got involved in this decision too.

Contact with RBMU came about because a friend of Geoff's had met a man called Herbert Pritchard on a train. Herbert and his wife, Betty, were working in a town called Muzaffarpur, Bihar Province, in North India and were looking for someone to get involved in ministry to students. There was also a hospital there for leprosy patients, which RBMU didn't run but supported with staff. Geoff contacted Herbert and Herbert suggested we talk to the RBMU HQ in London. We had various interviews with a variety of very worthy, elderly, somewhat out-of-touch, ex-missionaries. They felt that Geoff must have a year in church ministry in Britain. I needed to go to Bible college. That, I considered, was going to be challenging with my academic record.

Being at Grove Road Evangelical Church was no easy assignment. The congregation was large and well-off, but we were disappointed not to be given help getting a place to live. We ended up in a local bedsit, sharing the only bathroom with four other couples. Some days we had to go down to the church or to a railway station to use the loo.

Geoff was part-time at the church and not paid enough for us to live on. His wage was seven pounds a week and our rent five. So, he found another job. He worked two days a week at a gents' tailors in Walthamstow, a couple of miles along the North Circular – London's M25 at the time – delivering uniforms to private schools. I secured a place at the grandly named Mount Hermon Missionary Training College. This was in Ealing and the students (all women) lived at the college. However, the principal was very understanding and agreed I could live at home. So, I had a Tube train journey across London; an hour or more each way on the Central Line five days a week.

Six months into the course Geoff and I were facing the unexpected surprise of me being pregnant. Mark's arrival was not planned and cut across our intention to join RBMU. Also, I was well into my course and going to India depended on finishing. The daily journey to Ealing became too much. I moved into college and came home at weekends. I was separated from Geoff when I needed him most. Mind you, like the majority of males then, he needed someone to look after him. So, his eighty-plus-year-old granny came to stay in South Woodford and kept him fed, watered and in clean clothes.

That first year of marriage was not without other tensions. As I have mentioned, our living situation was stressful. Money was tight. Geoff's wages hardly matched our needs. I was paying to get to college each day. We had to go down the road to the launderette to wash our clothes and bedding. We didn't always have enough for food. One time, when I found we only had ten shillings for a week's groceries, I was distraught. I angrily grabbed the note and tore it into pieces and threw them at Geoff. In theory this was our first row, except that Geoff wasn't involved. He quietly picked up the shreds, stuck them together with Sellotape and went down to the bank to get the note exchanged for a new one.

I guess this illustrates that Geoff and I are very much a case of opposites attracting – an acute case, as it happens. Some years later we did a personality test and the comment made afterwards was that it was a wonder we had stayed together. Geoff is shy; I love being with people. Geoff is at the far end of the introvert scale; I am happily perched at the extreme end of EXTROVERT.

'Well,' we replied sweetly, 'we have had our difficulties.'

Nevertheless, we do share a lot in common. Our faith is precious to both of us. We like to travel. Geoff enjoys reading to me and I have never lost the joy of being read to. We both enjoy watching sport. Before our wedding Geoff had words of wisdom for me:

'You will have to learn about football and cricket, if we are going to have a good marriage.'

Cricket was fine. But not football. Early on, he took me to a game at Chelsea. Geoff yelled so much I was embarrassed to be with him. (Thank goodness he's an introvert!) I walked to the other end of the terrace and never went to another match.

As well as asking Geoff to pastor a church and me to study, RBMU wanted us to travel to churches around Britain, talking about what we were doing, raising prayer and financial support. We bought an old Austin A35 van, which we called 'Susie', for £150. She had a fold-down backseat, on which we put Mark's carry-cot. She drank a litre of oil every 100 miles and her heating system was broken. As the autumn chills set in, we drove with hot water bottles on our knees, but she just about got us from A to B and back again. Slowly – literally, travelling around in Susie – we were able to get all the equipment, ranging from a rucksack to a camp bed to a fridge (yes, you read that right), that RBMU had asked us to purchase. Geoff got hold of six oil drums and half a dozen crates and we began our packing for our placement in Muzaffarpur in earnest.

The biggest thing on our agenda that autumn was Mark's birth. I was in the middle of hosting a Tupperware party when things got serious. (Today's much maligned plastic was all the rage for beleaguered housewives then.) For the life of me I couldn't sit still. By 10 p.m. I knew I was going to have to call the party to a halt, send the Tupperware lady on her way, and get someone to haul Geoff out of a church meeting. I squeezed into Susie and off we stuttered into a foggy November night. When we got to the hospital, the doors were locked. I had to ring the bell several times before a nurse answered.

As was the way, Geoff was asked to hand over my case and told to go away. He could phone at 6 a.m. to see if he was a father. I was ushered into a side ward because the staff were busy, examined and told to sleep. I was soon giving the nurse hassle. I may have only done half a midwifery course, but I knew the contractions were too close together to ignore. Yes, she agreed, I was delivering Mark. Between contractions I had to walk down the corridors to the labour ward and, as a result, tore badly.

Mark was born with severe jaundice and two enormous bumps and blood clots on his head – probably the result of a fall I had suffered a couple of weeks earlier. The doctor whisked him away from me as soon as he arrived. We then endured a torrid ten days in the hospital where he was blood tested every day. Mark's clots, unusual in a baby, also attracted a lot of attention. Student doctors lined up regularly to discuss them. I chose to breast feed, the only one of twenty in the ward. The other women pronounced this 'disgusting' and insisted I drew the curtains around my bed. I think I cried more than Mark did those first ten days.

Come March 1965 we were packed and ready for India. Geoff's parents found it difficult to say goodbye. Geoff was their only son and Mark their only grandchild. They would see nothing of Mark's baby and toddler years. By the time we returned he would be five years old. Handwritten or typed letters, arriving once or twice a month, would be the only regular communication. I wouldn't say my father found it easier, it was just that we had been saying goodbye all our lives.

Our original sailing from Liverpool had been cancelled as the service had been discontinued. We and our luggage would have to travel by train across Europe to Venice. And when we landed in India? You guessed it. One of the first things we did was board another train.

Chapter 16

Under the Influence of Guinness

I could say that it was Guinness that got us to India. And I wouldn't be wrong, but probably I am thinking of a different Guinness than the one you are.

'Guinness' may have you picturing a glass of black dry stout wearing a heavy head of cream froth, a small golden harp, and a caption to tell you that the beer was first made in 1759 by Arthur Guinness, an Irish brewer of ales. Thereafter, the Guinness dynasty was assured fame, fortune, a certain amount of scandal, and a lot of TV advertising. What is less well known is that as well as brewers and bankers, the family also had its share of ministers and missionaries, among them one Revd. Henry Grattan Guinness, Doctor of Divinity, no less.

Henry was Arthur's grandson. He was born in Kingstown (now Dun Laoghaire), a small harbour town, just south of Dublin. That year – 1835 – Haley's Comet was doing its round of the night skies; as it happens its first appearance since 1759. His father, Captain John, an army officer in India, had suffered his shares of misfortune. Savage campaigns waged against Indian princes broke his health. On his return to Britain he lost his first wife and proved a poor businessman. He, therefore, retired on his army pension to the life of a Christian gentleman and not a great deal of income. In the circumstances, it is fortunate that he was the family's first teetotaller.

Henry's mother, Jane, had also lost a spouse. In tragic circumstances her first husband was killed in a reckless duel. She was eighteen, a mother of one daughter, and pregnant with a child who would be stillborn six months later. Left destitute, she contemplated suicide. In a strange incident she was saved from plunging herself into a river by the distraction of seeing a steady farmhand ploughing a nearby field. If, she told herself, he could be happy in such humble work, then, as best she could, she should make something of her life. Shortly afterwards, she dedicated herself more deeply to Jesus through the same Bible verse that had captivated George Muller: 'God so loved the world...'

Captain John and Jane married in 1829 and established the Guinness 'missionary' line – all three of their sons becoming ministers. However, it was Henry's younger brother who had a great influence on the direction of his life. Back from a sixteen-month voyage Wyndham told Henry the strange tale of the ship's chief mate, who had been mocked for his Christian beliefs by an abusive crew. However, while the seamen were clinging in terror to whatever they could in a storm that threatened to sink the ship, this man had knelt on deck and calmly asked God to still the storm. Remarkably, his prayers had been answered and Wyndham had been converted.

To cut a lengthy, but fascinating, story short, Henry devoted himself to God in a more meaningful way. He became a highly popular preacher; considered by some to be among the nineteenth century's three finest preachers. (The two others being D. L. Moody and Charles H. Spurgeon.) He travelled around Great Britain and Ireland, Europe, Canada and the USA, attracting thousands to hear him. In 1860 he married Fanny Fitzgerald, who had been brought up in the home of Quakers after the deaths of her parents. Twelve years on, one chill December evening, his wife found herself getting down from a horse-drawn tram into the grimy bustle of Mile End Road – half a mile from the hospital where I later worked – and being steered by her husband down an ugly passageway to stand in front of a rundown three-storey house.

'This is it?' she asked warily, her spirits sinking rapidly. 'This is where you want to start a missionary training college?'

'Yes!'

Their non-denominational college opened with six students. They went on to train over one thousand five hundred missionaries working with forty missions. They started churches and schools in the East End which ministered to around twelve thousand people a week. If that wasn't enough, they ran a mission yacht, and published a magazine they called, *Regions Beyond*.

About fifteen years later, Henry, Fanny and their son, Harry, established a missionary organisation with workers heading for central Africa; the Congo Balolo Mission. Then there were openings in Argentina and Peru. When Henry took a journey to the Far East with his daughter, Lucy, leading to missionaries being sent to North India, the organisation needed a new name: *Regions Beyond Missionary Union* – which brings me back, belatedly, to Geoff and I setting foot in Bombay (now Mumbai), the mission's newest and rawest recruits.

*****

The journey across Europe had gone well and we embarked on our ship in Venice as planned. As a child I had, of course, sailed through the Suez Canal before, but I found the experience just as enthralling. It felt like sailing across the desert sands; the channel so narrow that traders could throw baskets onto the deck. Some even managed to get on board, pressing us to buy, before being chased off again by the crew. There was an Indian couple on the ship, who helped us with our cultural orientation. They introduced us to Indian arranged marriage.

'In the West', they said, 'you fall in love and then marry. In India, we marry and then fall in love.'

The Bombay docks were wrapped in haze when we arrived and seemed the noisiest place on earth. An Indian approached me:

'Don't feed the baby,' he told me. 'Let him yell because Indians hate babies being allowed to cry. If he yells loud enough, you'll get through customs without any difficulty.'

So, we didn't feed Mark before we got off the ship. He cried his head off and, as predicted, the customs let us through with our oil drums and crates unchecked and without paying a rupee. (I have apologised to Mark since.)

Beyond the safety of customs, the hurly burly of Bombay buffeted us good and proper. I had Mark in a carrycot on wheels, trying to keep close to Geoff. The noise made it difficult to hear each other. Our noses were assailed with aromas we had never dreamt of. The heat wrung the sweat out of us. We were pushed and pulled in all directions and coolies grabbed at our bags and headed off we knew not where.

We were thankful for the RBMU agent, who guided us and another missionary couple out of the commotion and took us to find food. A curry was not what we needed, so we ordered egg and chips. Our fried eggs arrived first and then about thirty minutes later we got our chips – six each. Clearly, we were going to have to learn to enjoy Indian cuisine if we didn't want to go hungry. On that evening's train to Lucknow we did better, quickly picking up the system for getting food. We ordered what we wanted at one station, received our meals at the next, and handed back the empties at a third. It was at Lucknow that we nearly lost our oil drums and crates. Somehow, they ended up in a wagon that was being shunted onto another line. Geoff and our colleague agitatedly ran around, demanding that our freight went with us – which thankfully, it did.

As Geoff wrote to his Dad, the train engines were kept surprisingly 'spick and span', the carriages remarkably filthy, and the ride was particularly uncomfortable. We were jolted from Bombay to Lucknow, then Lucknow to

Muzaffarpur – roughly a thousand miles (without the innumerable bends) and a three-day journey. When we found the toilet, we discovered that it was a hole in the train floor – and that Indians don't use toilet paper! Instead, they clean themselves with their left hand, using running water, which is why, we discovered, they never touch food with that hand. We also learned that it is fine to use your fingers to pick up your food from your bowl, but only with your right hand, of course.

Delays were common. We sat in sidings waiting for other trains to pass on single track sections. At every level crossing, of which there were plenty, we were entertained by the train's ear-splitting whistle. Even more irritating was the driver blowing the whistle continually when we stopped at signals. It could be ten minutes or more before we moved on. Mark was not happy. When we arrived at Muzaffarpur, our friends had another fifty-mile stint to get to Motihari, but we were glad to be greeted by Herbert and Betty Pritchard and settle to sleep at their home, the Parsonage. We would be with them for around a month before we headed to the hills and began language study.

*****

Although India had become independent of Britain in 1947, nearly twenty years later it was hard to escape her colonial past. Our language school was in Landour, a village hidden beneath forest high in the Himalayan foothills – the so-called 'Queen of the Hills', not far from the Tibet border. This had been built at the behest of the British Army, a refuge from the rigours of the India heat. If Landour, at around seven thousand feet, usually tops the temperature charts at thirty degrees plus, Muzaffarpur, down on the plains, can hit the mid-forties and a high of more than fifty degrees.

There was little in Landour to suggest Indians had ever lived there. Apparently (and sadly), the British were keen to keep them out. The place was almost entirely made up of aging 'European' villas, with red roofs, white walls and verandahs. Even the name was derived from a Welsh place name, Llanddowror.

The village clings to a cliff, threaded together on the weave of ridiculously steep roads and impossible hairpin bends. Every morning we had to climb five hundred feet through the forest, from 'Edgehill', the suitably named missionary hostel where we lived, to Kellogg Memorial Church, a grey stone edifice with an amazing view of the mountains from its square turret. If that wasn't enough exercise for the day, there were a couple of dozen steps to be scaled before we made it through the church doors.

As well as being steep, the daily climb was lined with leeches that clung to our arms and legs as we brushed against leaves and grasses. The creatures were very adept at attaching themselves to our skin and it was a dickens of a job to remove them. Our hostess supplied us with little packets of salt. Dropping a pinch onto a leech usually did the trick, ensuring we arrived in class leech-free.

Each morning we had fifty minutes of grammar, fifty minutes of reading, and then fifty minutes of conversation, with time in a 'language lab' – rows of us recording on cumbersome reel to reel tapes, trying to perfect our pronunciation. Then back down the hill for lunch and another hour of private tuition. Since both of us had to study, Mark had an Indian *ayah* to look after him.

Hindi was hard. Geoff and I progressed, generally in fits and starts – but mainly in fits...

For a start there were forty-six letters. What do you do with four 'd's and four 't's (none of which sounded anything like an English 'd' or 't')? It was all in the breathing we learned. Or didn't as the case may be. Geoff once preached a sermon on the Bible story of Jesus and the blind egg (instead of the blind man)!

The good news was that each letter had only one way of saying it (unlike an 'a' or 'e' in English). Once learned, reading became easy. We could stand alongside the most fluent Hindi speakers and sing hymns and read prayers nearly as well as they could. They, no doubt, understood what they were saying. We had no idea.

Writing was interesting. Hindi (or Devanagari, to give it the correct name) letters have wonderful shape – curves and straights fastened together in elaborate squiggles. Put them together and you have a word. However, before we were allowed to do that, we had to make our own quills. Those were the days.

Geoff, bless him, was a very precise plodder. He had to know exactly how to pronounce a phrase before he would say anything – even if he still got it incorrect from time to time. I, on the other hand, had no problems making mistakes. Spending a good proportion of my time with children was useful. If I got something wrong, they would just laugh and correct me. I found it easier to learn sentences off pat and then trot them out when required. I still remember one of the first phrases we were given, '*Mali, tum kahan ho*?' – Gardener, where are you? (More colonialism!) Not an altogether useless phrase. We did have a gardener in Muzaffarpur, a Muslim young man, and no doubt I was happy to ask him where he was from time to time. My trouble was the grammar. I didn't understand English grammar. So, Geoff had to teach me that first, before I could learn where to put Hindi adjectives, nouns and verbs in a sentence.

One of the wonderful sights in Landour was to gaze across magnificent hills and stunning valleys to the Himalayas, heavy with snow or shrouded in cloud. A breath-taking picture postcard view, if ever there was one. It was a spectacle frequently disturbed by a succession of students shuffling past, their gaze firmly fixed on the ring of cards in their hand, the magic broken by their muttering, over and over, the words on the cards. These hundred cards held our future. Once learned, we were given another hundred. At the end of our stay we would be tested orally and, if we passed, when we returned to Landour the following spring, we would be allowed to tackle the next level.

In September, we did just that and returned to Muzaffarpur feeling pleased with ourselves. For the rest of the year we would study with a private tutor. Now it was time to really get to grips with living and working in India.

Chapter 17

Early Days

I said earlier that Geoff and I were the rawest of recruits when we arrived in Bombay. This was true. Neither of us spoke a smidgen of Hindi. We knew little about Hinduism or Islam. As to Indian culture, that was a complete conundrum. In the first few months I was forever making tea for guests, only for them to leave as soon as they arrived. I was puzzled and put out. It seemed rude to say the least. Eventually, someone pointed out that serving tea was a polite way of asking visitors to leave!

We had received next to no orientation from RBMU. The best advice I got for caring for a four-month-old baby in a foreign country – or, for that matter, any problems we were likely to encounter – was 'just manage'. I was fortunate to have my nursing training, because Mark was too young for a lot of his jabs when we left England. I could have done with more help, but 'good missionary training' often meant suffering and surviving, not getting practical information.

Geoff was worried about the food. His family were very much 'meat and two veg'. A friend had taken him to the Indian Embassy in London, where there was a restaurant. Invited to bite into a chilli, it had burnt his mouth. I was less concerned. As a child I was used to rice and Asian recipes. Also, Mageen had been raised in Kuala Lumpur, so she made an English version of curry. On the other hand, Geoff had known some Indian students at London Bible College. I may have had a patient or two from India or Pakistan, but had never got to do much more than change their sheets and take their temperatures.

We were fortunate to stay with the Pritchards on arrival. They had been in Muzaffarpur for three or four years and in India for decades before that. Betty was, in fact, the senior missionary. She had arrived in the country way back in 1930, before we were born, in the days when women missionaries wore pith helmets and out-of-the-Ark long dresses. How they coped with the heat is beyond me.

Betty had been brought up in Preston and was, according to her own assessment, short on patience, and fanned into flame by stupidity. Blunt, I'd have said. She also described herself as a 'whatnot'; a useful part of the mission, but not really noticed. In reality, she was mistaken. She was a valuable asset to RBMU. Although she had started out as an evangelist, telling people about Jesus, and been involved in dispensing medicine, by the time we arrived she had found a role for herself that bore fruit way beyond the borders of Bihar Province.

Since the birth of her daughter, she had been increasingly frustrated by deafness, forced to wear a clumsy device – earphones, with a battery in a box as big as a Bible – that just got in the way; a hindrance as much as an aid. (Actually, this was something of an advantage to us. When Herbert was away, we could allow Mark to yell his head off and not worry. Betty couldn't hear him!) One day she had prayed in desperation that God would show her what on earth she could possibly do without using her ears. Something – anything – that could be significant. Within a few hours she had picked up a magazine and found an advert for a writing competition. The winning Christian novel would be published in English by the All India Book Club and then in regional languages. Betty won and that started her writing career good and proper. Using an Indian pen name, Asha, her books and articles were now being read across the country and RBMU was more than happy to promote her work to an even wider audience.

Although Betty was old enough to be my mother, we had more in common than we may have expected. She had raised two children in India, a girl and a boy – I had the boy and a girl was less than a couple of years away. Her daughter was my age and a nurse. We had both attended Mount Hermon College and she had done language study at Landour.

It was at Landour that Betty and Herbert had met. He was just finishing his studies and she was taking a break from her work with the Bible Churchman's Missionary Society (now Crosslinks) at a hospital in the province next to ours, Uttar Pradesh. Due to suffering polio as a child, she had difficulty crossing rocks en route to a picnic. She had arrived bruised and feeling fragile. He, gallantly, had brought water, washed her wounds, and applied plasters. Their hands touched and their future was sorted. Well, in a manner of speaking. They had an interesting relationship. He was from Northern Ireland, an upright Quaker, patience personified. She, as she said, was as impatient as an alarm clock. Perhaps Geoff and I had more in common with them than we liked to admit?

By the time we arrived in Muzaffarpur, Herbert was the most senior male RBMU missionary in India and was, alongside two others, running the show. In the mission he was praised for his perseverance; getting difficult things done, even if he had no training. He had also obtained quite a formidable reputation amongst some of the Indians he had helped. One, no doubt, he didn't want. Unable to obtain medicine on three occasions from the dispensary Betty and Herbert ran, a man told his wife to gather up the dust where Herbert had walked. Obediently, she had done so. Remarkably, he had eaten it. Astonishingly, he had got better!

Shortly after our arrival, Geoff fell seriously ill with vomiting and diarrhoea. No medicine seemed to help. He lost a lot of weight. Herbert and Betty called in the Civil Surgeon, the top doctor in the area. It was not good news. He told us that there was nothing that could be done for Geoff. He was, he said, 'a goner'. You can imagine how I felt. We'd been married less than two years and here I was in India with a five-month-old child. Then Herbert and Betty made a suggestion. The dispensary they'd run for twenty years had been a homeopathic one, in reality the only affordable treatment for the poor local people. Tentatively, Betty asked me if they could give Geoff a remedy they called 'corpse reviver'. Although my training had been in orthodox western medicine, I was so desperate that I was ready to try anything.

'Yes, of course,' I said.

It proved an effective decision. From that day onwards Geoff began to recover.

The Parsonage, the Pritchards' bungalow home, belonged to the 'British' church next door – Christ Church, part of the United Church of Northern India. Its design was quite outlandish, designed with an eccentric mix of ecclesiastical arches, castle battlements, and nearly two dozen mini-turrets. The Parsonage was far less showy; large and long, with a flat roof, wooden shuttered windows, and a wide tiled verandah. Both buildings had thick, rendered, off-white walls, which were in desperate need of a good coat of paint.

The church was as interesting inside as it was quirky to us, with our upbringing in British churches and chapels, on the outside. At the end of each pew were slots for rifles. Lining the walls were dozens of brass plaques commemorating Brits who had died; soldiers in the Boer and First World Wars, tea planters killed in accidents, and not a few wives, some of them as young as eighteen.

When the last British pastor left Muzaffarpur, the Bishop had agreed to rent the church to RBMU. We were allowed to use the church for services as long as we said the Creed, prayed the Lords' Prayer, and had Sunday's Collect. With Herbert a Quaker, Geoff an evangelical Baptist, and Betty with her Methodist background playing the harmonium, it made for unusually ecumenical services.

This part of town was definitely 'colony'. On the other side of the Parsonage from the church was the Civil Surgeon's house and across the lilac coloured gravel of the driveway beyond the tamarind trees and a gorgeous frangipani lived the Commissioner, the Senior District Officer and the Chief Engineer. These huge residences and any number of bungalows all fronted on to the *Maidan* – what we would call a common. When the British 'ruled', it had been a racecourse and used for polo matches. These unspoilt acres were sacrosanct as far as building was concerned. So much so that the railway line looped all the way around them, adding several minutes to a journey.

In the early morning of the hot season the *Maidan* was a marvellous place to walk and enjoy the flowering trees, a cascade of vibrant colours. But once the sun rose much above the horizon, a heat haze descended and a sweltering west wind stoked up a furnace. It was better to be inside and wait for the cooler evening breezes. These, unfortunately, brought out the mosquitos and bugs ready to do battle with anyone foolish enough to sit out on their verandah. I fairly quickly adopted Punjabi dress – a sari and baggy trousers – as my defence and we retreated behind nets and screens. Needless to say, when dealing with a crying baby at night, the mozzies were always going to win.

*****

After our first session of language study at Landour, we didn't return to live with the Pritchards. We moved into a small property that had been done up for us. This was far less grand and on a new estate, a couple of miles from the Parsonage and on the other side of the railway station. In translation it had an amusing address: Majhaulia house, near the graveyard, Cowshed Road, City of Mosquitos. Nevertheless, it did bring us more into contact with Indian neighbours. We were the first RBMU personnel to live in the local community, rather than on a mission compound.

Our new home was a semi-detached bungalow, but when we arrived, we discovered that our Muslim neighbours were building a second storey above us. We were blessed with a verandah at the front and another out the back, looking onto a courtyard and trees, where Mark could play safely and we could sleep if we wished. Both of our bedrooms had ceiling fans, which were very welcome. The toilet, however, was Indian – squat style, which took a while to get used to; just one of the countless things that challenged our comfort zones in those early days.

Each morning we were up around 5 a.m. to enjoy as much of the cool dawn as we could. Breakfast on the verandah was *sooji* – a semolina porridge, which for those raised on Sixties and Seventies school dinners may not sound a great way to start the day – with chapattis, butter and marmalade. Our butter came from buffalo milk because the buffalos didn't get TB – or so we were told. Every day we had milk delivered. I boiled it and scooped off the cream. We then beat the cream into butter and added a mustard seed to make it look yellow. The marmalade I made from the pomelos and lemons on the trees around our home.

After breakfast and family prayers we went in different directions for a while. Geoff was involved with students. He worked out of a Christian bookshop on a wide busy street in the bazaar, the last in a row of small stores run by local families. There were no shopfront windows and doors. Accordion shutter doors were pushed back and wares spilled over onto the pavement. Owners spent their days catching the attention of passers-by, whether they happened to be on foot, in rickshaws, or riding bicycles and motorcycles.

Geoff's shop had wide open blue doors and wooden racks on which he and his Indian colleague – a young man named John Mathew – laid out booklets, pamphlets and tracts, alongside college and school books. Students were always keen to learn English and would frequently drop by to talk to Geoff. Sometimes he took Mark with him to the store. When Mark began talking, he proved a popular chatterbox. In the back of the shop there was another quite successful work going on. Geoff and John ran a correspondence course, where students could 'earn' a New Testament and then a Bible. In addition, at her home, another RBMU missionary, Aza Child, was translating Bible notes into Hindi. These were being sent out to over a thousand Indian Christians.

I cycled to the hospital run by the Leprosy Mission, where I did the morning round of injections. Leprosy was a huge problem out in the villages. Our British doctor regularly went into the countryside, working with the *Panchayat* – the village elders. She taught people to spot tell-tale patches and encouraged early treatment. Outpatients came to the hospital for help day in and day out. However, there were also about fifty residents, patients who had been thrown out of their homes. They earned their keep by doing jobs – cooking, sweeping the floor, and making shoes from old tyres because damage to feet was a real problem for people with the disease. One of them boiled up the glass syringes and sharpened the needles ready for my arrival. Then I made my way around the ward, stopping at bed mat after bed mat.

There was a lot of ignorance about medicine in those days and India's cultural norms only added to the problem. We charged a little for the tablets and potions. If we didn't, people would throw them away, thinking they were worthless. Towards the end of our time in India Geoff was working as business manager at the hospital. One day he was called to deal with an angry man who was buying medication. He had been given the same drug, dapsone, as a low caste man.

'I don't want the same medicine as this street dweller,' he was shouting at the dispenser. 'I want better medicine. I can pay more.'

Geoff, patiently, explained there was only one medicine for all leprosy sufferers, regardless of age, caste, religion or social standing.

'Huh, it's only for my wife. I won't buy it,' he stormed, 'It is cheaper for me to get another wife.' And with that he stomped off.

That was a bad day. However, the hospital did have a valuable impact on the community and helped a huge number of sufferers and their families. Something it continues to do. Remarkably, the Leprosy Mission is still running the hospital it started as a small home in Muzaffarpur for leprosy 'refugees' over a hundred years ago.

My time at the hospital was shorter than I may have expected. The staff were keen for me to work there fulltime, but the mission felt I should devote more time to language study and, with the Pritchards going on home leave, Betty's hospitality role had to be maintained. Plus, I was about to have a baby and she certainly needed to be my priority.

Chapter 18

Long Distance Labour

If getting to the hospital on time to have Mark was an ordeal, having Rachel in January 1968 was a whole different chapter of events. And the saga started before she was even conceived.

The mission had strict rules on babies. Just as there were regulations on when you could get married (RBMU's permission was needed), so babies could not be born at willy-nilly times that pleased their parents. We were not allowed to have another child until we had passed our second language exam – pressure to pass or what! The day I got my (successful) results back was the day we abandoned contraception.

The next issue was where was I to have the baby. Mission protocol demanded that a local maternity unit would not do. I must travel five hours north on the train – coal grit, smuts, jolting, endless whistling and all – to the town of Raxaul, where RBMU had a hospital.

From the mission's point of view Raxaul was a very strategic place to work, sitting as it does on the Nepalese border and running the only train line into the country. In fact, the railway station, being built around the time RBMU arrived in 1926, was a very cosmopolitan place. Gurkha soldiers jostled with pilgrims and traders. And, of course, the occasional burdened missionary wife seeking a bed in which to deliver her baby and not looking forward to her impending labour at all.

I had been there once for a check-up earlier in my pregnancy, but cared for myself subsequently. Come the due date, Geoff, Mark – now, just two – and I got hard wooden seats on the train and arrived at the hospital only to be informed that they were busy and didn't have any spare accommodation. Geoff was told to catch the next train back to Muzaffarpur with Mark, while I stayed. Poor Geoff. That was twice he got no further than the hospital doors!

Perhaps unsurprisingly, considering the bumpy rail ride to Raxaul, I had Rachel the next day. I felt rough in the morning, had crippling back pain after lunch, and by tea it was worse. In spite of my training, I couldn't believe I was in labour, but my doctor friend said (as only women in authority can do):

'Come on, my girl... if we don't go now, we'll be too late.'

I waddled down to the hospital and an hour later I was holding Rachel in my arms.

Next morning Geoff had just finished his breakfast when there was a knock on the door. It was the man from the telegraph office carrying a telegram from Rachel. She wanted her dad. Geoff, unusually, ran around in an excited flap, trying to gather up stuff, change Mark, cobble together lunch, and call a rickshaw *wallah* more or less all at the same time. Then, he and Mark were on the 10.15 a.m. train heading north again.

We had three nights in Raxaul together and then I was informed I could leave. At less than four days old, Rachel got her first Indian train ride – and Geoff and Mark had their fourth journey on a wooden seat in six days.

Rachel aroused a great deal of local interest. Our Indian neighbours were curious to see her and we were often stopped in the bazaar by strangers. They were baffled at her hair colour – Geoff and I were both dark.

'Why has she got white hair?' was a common question.

'Is she a granny or is she a child?' was another.

'Can we borrow your soap?' They wanted to be 'white' like my daughter.

While it may have sounded exotic to be born in India, it later caused Rachel a lot of problems. Like others born overseas, she and I were both classed as 'aliens'. It took a lot of huffing and puffing from prominent people, whose parents had been in the army or diplomatic service, to get the government to change that. More difficult was the reaction she got when she went to school in Britain. Girls decided she was from Pakistan, despite her protests that she had been born in India. The less kind called her a 'Paki', which was very offensive to Pakistanis, let alone her.

Two months after Rachel's birth, the Pritchards returned to the UK on a short home leave. They moved out of the Parsonage, allowing us to move back in. Their absence meant that Geoff had to take on Herbert's roles, particularly vital as a new hospital building was nearing completion. Picking up Betty's hospitality role created a major change for me as well. Muzaffarpur was a stop along the route for a lot of folk. We had our fair share of missionaries coming through, heading to Motihari and Raxaul, often needing a rest from train travel, even if it was for just a few hours.

We also had a large number of hippies – wandering through India, looking for their own interpretation of heaven, hoping to find it in a Himalayan 'Shangri-La'. To be frank, they were often not the nicest people on earth and may well not have been allowed in if the place existed. For some reason many seemed to think that India owed them an existence and were quick to demand it. A number didn't smell too great either. I had a policy of providing a meal, a shower, and room on the verandah to sleep. The guest bedrooms were off limits. The less fortunate ones were directed (not by us) to the Roman Catholic Convent down the road, where, according to Betty, the Austrian Sister Superior, Eleanora, gave them a 'loving but exceedingly bracing' welcome.

One of the good things about living at the Parsonage was that we could hear the early morning train as it approached the town. We then had plenty of time to get up and drive the few minutes to the rear entrance of the station as the train laboriously chuffed all the way around the *Maidan* to its destination. Mark and Rachel really loved this. A trip out in

134

their pyjamas was a real adventure. When our visitors tumbled sleepily out of the jeep, breakfast was waiting for them on the verandah. With a little practice we timed this routine to perfection.

We were fortunate to inherit both the bungalow and the Pritchard's cook, a delightful Indian man called Gahar, who had been with them for around twenty years and was very familiar with the peculiarities of the British. We were less blessed by some of the Indians with whom we had dealings, although we did take things in good humour. The buffalo milk got increasingly watery as time went on until I had words with the milkman. Next day it would be restored to its full richness... but only for a while. On one occasion, I spotted someone wearing my sari in the bazaar. I knew it was mine because I had bought the material in Delhi and no-one locally had the same. The washerman denied it belonged to me. It was then I realised that the reason we didn't get our clothes back from the laundry for a week was because they were being washed, loaned to others, and then washed again.

I tried growing fruit and vegetables, but this proved exceedingly frustrating. Not infrequently, when something was just ready for harvesting, it would disappear overnight. We had more success in loaning out a field behind the house to a local farmer. He grew lentils and gave us half the crop. I remember one time watching him ploughing with two oxen. One of the beasts broke free from the yoke and lumbered off, leaving the other going around in circles, while the farmer gave chase. A sermon illustration, if ever there was one (see Matthew 11:29, if you are interested).

What vegetables I did salvage, we put on the roof to dry. We would climb up on a rickety bamboo ladder and lay them out on the tiles – beans, cabbages, cauliflowers, tomatoes and the like. These made their way into Gahar's curries, which we had at lunch. After lunch everyone went to bed for an hour or two. In the heat a siesta was the best use of anyone's time. It did mean that life went on longer in the evenings though. After supper – curry again, of course – Geoff went back to his bookshop, which stayed open until 10 p.m.

*****

If negotiating our way around Indian ways of life was at times as tricky as the hairpin bends up to Landour, our encounters with the wildlife could be unsettling to say the least. Particularly when keeping the natural world out of your home was impossible. Still, what was perturbing then, makes for some good stories now.

Let me start with the rats; a regular feature in missionary tales.

One night I woke and complained to Geoff that he had woken me up. This he denied, insisting that it was the other way around. I was about to say I was certainly in the right, when I spotted a rat sitting on the bedhead. It was pulling at Geoff's hair through the fine holes in the mosquito net, wanting it for a nest. Another time, I reached for the Tupperware box in which I kept five year's supply of tampons. (I had brought them from Britain. You couldn't buy sanitaryware in our part of India back then.) There was a hole in the side of it. When I lifted the lid, I discovered a rat's nest in there, with ten babies in it. They had eaten all the tails off my tampons. Consequently, I had to throw the lot away and ask Geoff's Dad to send me some more.

It was very easy for rats to get into the house. Every room had small drainage holes in the walls to allow the cleaner to wash down the floors and get rid of the dirty water. We put poison in the holes, but inevitably it didn't always work. To be honest, in the wet season the frogs were less welcome than the rats. There was nothing worse than settling down for the night – except perhaps mosquitos – and hearing a frog croaking somewhere in the room. There were many occasions when we played 'hunt the amphibian', looking under wardrobes and chests of drawers, before we got any sleep.

Scorpions? They could be a problem in and out of doors. We were always careful to put our shoes inside our mosquito nets at night. No-one wants to put their bare foot on a scorpion first thing in the morning, do they? Once Geoff tried to kill one. The scorpion was not amused. It chased him around and around the courtyard at our home for some time. I wondered who was chasing whom!

And then there were the snakes.

The worst snake was a krait, a black snake with white stripes, about three feet long, which is particularly poisonous. They mainly come out at night and had a cunning knack of wrapping themselves around light switches. On one occasion, we had a cobra – longer than a krait and with its distinctive hood – turn up in the Parsonage garden. Gahar and our gardener rushed out to deal with it. What we hadn't realised though was that the snake had a mate. For a time afterwards this snake kept appearing around the property. In the end we had to get someone in to take care of it for us. The risks to the children were just too great.

This, unfortunately, was not the nearest we got to a brush with death. There were two occasions when we could have come off very badly indeed. The first involves an elephant. I'll leave the second incident for the next chapter.

Early on, Geoff and I were invited along with five or six others to go to a *mela*. Betty kindly agreed to care for Mark and the leprosy hospital doctor drove the Bedford ambulance for our day out. As well as being a Hindu festival, an event attended by millions of people, the *mela* was an enormous market. In some respects, it was like one of our county shows. Handicrafts and cuisine from all over India were being sold in booths. However, in addition to cattle, donkeys and horses, there were elephants and monkeys on show.

The market was fascinating. We wandered around the stalls and tasted the different foods, until we came near to the elephant enclosures. Suddenly, we were engulfed in screams. One of the elephants had broken free. Our doctor friend yelled at us to huddle together as the crowd panicked and fled in our direction. We were buffeted and battered, but our group held firm until the animal was caught. After that we just went home, shocked by the news that about thirty people had died in the stampede.

It wasn't just wildlife that disrupted our lives. Periodically, the cows on the *Maidan* would wander into the garden and take to eating our flowers. I was not best pleased. Gahar taught our black mongrel, Tigger, to hang onto their tails (I am not sure how he did this) and then chase them back out the gate. From time to time passers-by would hear me shouting:

'Tigger! *Gay hai*!'

and a few moments later a number of cows would go lumbering back across Chakkar Road onto the safety of the *Maidan*.

Chapter 19

Balancing Act

When RBMU chose to work in north India, it didn't pick the easiest place to try and teach people about Jesus and establish churches. Herbert said that he had been preaching in Bihar for twenty years and hadn't seen a single convert.

The province was highly religious. The Hindu goddess, Sita, was said to have been born in Bihar. The Buddha, Siddhartha Gautama himself, had sat under a bodhi tree south of Muzaffarpur and, according to Buddhist tradition, been enlightened. Nepal and its form of Buddhism was just across the border. (When we were in Landour, we had seen the Dalai Lama on his visit to a school.) All around us were hundreds of thousands of Hindus and Muslims, the majority being Hindus. Plus, there were followers of the Jain religion, another of India's ancient religions. To say that Christians were not welcome in Muzaffarpur would be an exaggeration, but it was not always a safe place to be.

Geoff had a lot of students come to the bookshop. They were eager to learn about what to them was a strange religion. Many said that they believed in Jesus and I have no reason to doubt them. However, Hindus had little problem in adding an extra god to the dozens they already had. It was getting baptised that was a sticking point. Even though Indian pastors would do this in streams away from the villages, the students feared their parents would reject them or their wives would leave them. Geoff knew only one student who decided to go ahead. As a result, his wife and his father both threatened suicide and he was thrown out of his village. Nevertheless, these difficulties did not deter him in his faith. He later worked with Operation Mobilisation in India.

Sadly, there could also be more serious consequences. Although we never had problems at Christ Church, the Indian pastor at the Methodist Church in Muzaffarpur was under severe pressure to move on. His predecessor had been beaten up and left. Assassins had been hired to kill this new pastor. His wife and children lived in terror of what may happen to him and to them.

Some years before, in another part of Bihar, Betty and Herbert had known a Brahmin (a member of the superior caste in India), who had become a Christian and been baptised. He had been forced to leave home and find menial work. When he visited his family, stones were thrown at him. His mother placed food outside the house, treating him like a beggar. Once, he said, he was sure she had poisoned the meal. When the persecution began to affect his wife, he left the district. This man's example and preaching had led a farmer, another Brahmin, to study Christianity. Eager to learn, he lived in Betty and Herbert's compound for a while. One day he asked them if he could be baptised. They were more than happy to say 'yes', but that afternoon he went to the bazaar and never returned. They could only conclude that he had been killed for his faith.

There were, however, many good things to reflect on. RBMU's work, through its hospitals, schools and an orphanage at Motihari, was very effective in relieving suffering and helping the less fortunate. The Muzaffarpur leprosy hospital was a godsend for the fifty or so inpatients. They had been ostracised by their families and community. Life could have been one long despair of days, spent in filthy rags, sitting on the pavement, waiting for a passer-by to chuck a coin in their direction. Instead, they found shelter and love and a new faith, which gave them hope. Remarkably, some even went so far as to say that they were glad they had leprosy, otherwise they would never have got to know Jesus.

Going to the Kanhauli Church at the hospital was a great experience. The church was small but vibrant. From time to time there were baptisms. (No-one cared too much whether people with leprosy were baptised.) The church, named after the local district, was made up of patients and staff, singing Hindi *bhajans* – heartily, though not necessarily tunefully. Any new hymns were learned, practised around fires at night, and then sung at the next service, often completely unrecognizable from the original.

Christ Church, our church on the *Maidan*, largely attracted Indian Christians who had travelled from South India where Christianity was strong. The Methodist Church in town was much larger, having around one hundred at services on a Sunday, while Christ Church had fifty or so members. Not big numbers in a city of a hundred thousand, but these were churches with strong congregations. In spite of the opposition, it was encouraging to see people learning and growing in their faith through the preaching, Bible studies and prayer meetings.

The other congregation that was alive and well in Muzaffarpur was that of the Roman Catholics. Sister Superior Eleanora, from the convent of Indian nuns near the Parsonage, became a real friend of ours. When the Pritchards arrived in the city, the two denominations never passed the time of day until, unexpectedly, Sister Eleanora breezed into their home and announced:

'Isn't it lovely we can now be friends?'

The Pope had given Roman Catholics permission to talk to Protestants.

Eleanora had a sad story to tell us. During the Second World War she had been running a home for about twenty Down's Syndrome children in Austria. When the Nazis turned up at the doors, they shot all the children in front of her. Appalled and grieving she had left Europe and made her home in India.

She was quite a remarkable person. Coming from a peasant family, she was brusque and down to earth, but delightfully kind. She was unfortunate to only have one kidney and that didn't function too well. Even so, she was a force to be reckoned with. As well as keeping her convent and nuns in order, she was running a school for about a thousand pupils, dealing with the beggars who thronged the gates of the convent, and bartering with traders and workmen who were not used to her Austrian efficiency.

One of the doctors at the hospital taught her to drive, which may have been a mistake. Woe betide anyone or any animal that dared to get in her way as she drove through the bazaar. She just put her foot down and kept going. We had this saying, 'There goes Jehu', as she roared past the gates of the Parsonage.

On her visits we used to pray with her. She and Geoff had Bible studies together. I think she was shocked to discover that Protestants and Roman Catholics did not always agree on theology. She made a point of not talking about Mary with us. She was also very touchy on the subject of purgatory – a half-way house between earthly life and heaven, where people are made pure before entering Paradise. As Protestants we don't believe purgatory exists. She was quite upset to think that she would have to go there and we wouldn't!

There was no doubting that Sister Eleanora had a very real faith. One day, a well-dressed couple with two small children came to the Parsonage. They said they had been robbed on the train and had no money to continue their long-distance journey to get work. Could we help them with money for new tickets? Geoff and I looked at each other. Money was in short supply at the time. We would have been left with next to nothing for the rest of the month. We gave them something to drink and then headed to our bathroom to pray. Should we give them the money or not?

As we emerged, Sister Eleanora came tearing up the drive in clouds of dust.

'I was going to the bazaar,' she told us, 'and God said that I had to visit the Larcombes. And I said to God, "I'm sorry, God, I haven't got time to see the Larcombes today." And God said, "Go and see the Larcombes!"'

Apparently, she had argued with God for about five minutes. But he had been insistent. So, she had come to see us.

When she walked in and saw the couple, she was furious.

'I've just given you the money for your tickets…' she scolded them. She sent them away with fleas in their ears.

Brusque, but lovely!

*****

Once we had settled into Muzaffarpur, got our Hindi sorted to a point where Geoff could preach regularly, we could chat with our Indian friends, neighbours and traders, and we became less bothered by the weather, life became comfortable. Mark and Rachel were happy. The Parsonage's large garden was perfect for them to play in and they were young enough to enjoy the fuss they got as foreign children.

After Rachel was born, Herbert was away for six months, with Betty staying on in the UK for a longer period. While the Parsonage was being converted into two homes, Herbert moved in with us. To be honest we were glad when Betty arrived back about ten weeks later. Herbert on his own wasn't always easy to live with. He brought back cassette tapes of his son, Mike, preaching and played them enthusiastically to visitors. They were good, but you can have too much of a good thing. He also talked about Mike constantly, to the point we were beginning to get inferiority complexes.

There was also a problem over meals. Herbert didn't really like Indian food, though he protested he did. As our senior missionary we catered more to his likes, but we – and Mark in particular – did miss Gahar's curries. Once Betty came, she and Herbert took up residence in one half of the Parsonage and we became neighbours; an arrangement that suited us all. We were able to re-establish our family life, eat curry to our hearts' content, and listen to our own tapes.

Our finances were always a bit of a balancing act. Before we left the UK, we had raised funds through our church visits. Once in India, we received an allowance from RBMU each month. The full amount was just about sufficient for day to day costs, but it certainly didn't cover extras. Needless to say, with workers in the Congo, Nepal, Peru, and the Indonesian half of New Guinea (then called Irian Jaya), there wasn't always enough in RBMU's kitty and frequently we got less than the full amount.

One month we got nothing at all. Mother Hubbard-like, my cupboard was bare. However, when the post arrived, very unusually, there was an airmail letter that had made the journey by sea. Inside was a timely cheque for fifty pounds, ten pounds more than our allowance. This had come from a nurse in the South Woodford church whom we hardly knew. I was all for restocking my larder with the whole lot. Geoff, however, said we should share it with another family, who were in a similar plight to ourselves. The following month a funfair owner in the USA, hearing about the mission's predicament, sent a cheque to cover all RBMU's allowances. Two very different people, used by God to supply our needs, to whom we were very grateful.

Away from the sanctuary of the *Maidan* Muzaffarpur was not as peaceful as we would have liked. Hindus and Muslims seemed to be at loggerheads much of the time and there were riots now and again. One year there was an Anti-English campaign. We had to remove signs at the hospital and the bookshop and put up Hindi ones. There was nothing to do except lay low for a while until life went back to normal.

Our first Christmas was particularly memorable. Geoff and I decided a week or two in advance to go to the bazaar to do our Christmas shopping. We called a rickshaw and set out. However, instead of the normal chaos of the Indian streets – goats, rickshaws, bicycles, motorcycles, humans, cars, cows, more rickshaws, more humans, yet more rickshaws (we were told there were four thousand rickshaws on the roads) – we found ourselves being carted through a ghost town. All the shops were shut. The quiet was eerie.

A few minutes later, we found ourselves looking at the wrong end of a rifle. A jeep screeched to a halt in front of us and a police officer demanded to know where we thought we were going.

'Christmas shopping…' we said rather weakly.

'Go home… now!' he ordered and then laid into the rickshaw *wallah* for bringing us out.

'Don't you know there is a curfew? We've been told to shoot on sight.'

There had been a protest at the university. A teacher and a student had been killed when the police opened fire. We had heard vans with loudhailers announcing something, but our Hindi was not good enough to know what was being said. We didn't get our Christmas shopping done that evening, but, mercifully, we did survive to tell the tale.

We had other problems with the authorities. The year after we arrived, missionaries were required to get a special residential visa. Every year we reapplied and had a nervous wait until our permits were issued. There was a lot of anti-British feeling in some quarters. The government talked about getting rid of missionaries. A number of provinces, including Bihar, proposed 'Freedom of Religion' Acts. Converting anyone would be an offence and pastors would have to register the names of believers they baptised. Things got tense. Reprisals were possible. For a short while RBMU decided everyone should stop language study and get on with their mission work, since it looked like we wouldn't be staying long. We had to have a suitcase ready for evacuation. Thankfully, we made it through to our home leave in 1971.

As we left Muzaffarpur, it was a good time to review our five years in India. As a family we had arrived with one child and with Rachel's arrival we felt very complete. Mark was now at the Roman Catholic Montessori School and his sister was catching up. Workwise, we had seen a lot of progress. The churches continued to be a blessing, despite their ups and downs. I had been involved with the leprosy patients and then kept dozens of travellers fed, watered and sheltered. The new hospital was complete and in good health, in part due to Geoff's involvement in the management. He had also been asked to join the leadership team of RBMU in Bihar.

The bookshop was doing particularly well. Geoff had introduced a lot of fresh ideas and trained up John Mathew to run it. John was also eager to try new things. Sales were increasing. Students were involved in regular Bible studies. Over four hundred were enrolled on the correspondence courses. Now local Christians were involved and looking at ways to make the Literature Centre, as we now called it, self-supporting.

We knew we would miss Muzaffarpur. Still, our break was only for a year. Or so we thought. The reality was that we were not coming back to India any time soon. I didn't visit Muzaffarpur for another thirty-six years.

Chapter 20

Hard Times

Rachel and I arrived back in the UK in February 1971. Not the best time to put in an appearance as it turned out. While I had been away, people had seen a man standing on the moon, but Britain was on the brink of a dismal decade. Workers on strike, three day working weeks, electricity shortages, no sugar in the shops, and no petrol in the pumps were all in waiting. There was a lot of talk about joining Europe in a Common Market. Plus, shillings had just been replaced with decimal currency. Now we were looking at one hundred pence to a pound and losing half pence pieces at the bottom of our purses. Oh, and it was snowing and I had no coat.

Actually, the situation was worse than that. In India we had received a telegram to say Geoff's mother had suffered a stroke. No more than that. We didn't have a phone and neither did my parents-in-law. We knew she had been having blood pressure problems, but our last news was that she was out of hospital and things were under control. Now, we had no idea if she was alive or dead. Geoff and I agreed I should come back with Rachel and see what needed to be done. He and Mark would fly back as planned in March, at the end of our five years of service.

It was an anxious trip down to Minehead. I found Geoff's Mum alive. She was on the way to recovery, but still very unwell. His Dad was in fulltime work and was trying to care for her. I moved into the family home and set about running the house, as well as settling Rachel into her new environment. The poor girl had never been anywhere as cold as Britain in her life.

Similarly, Mark, now five, was going to have to make a lot of adjustments. He and Geoff landed at Heathrow Airport in torrential rain and were taken to Geoff's aunt and uncle's home in Watford for the first night. Mark would not settle to sleep, because someone had apparently forgotten to put up his mosquito net. He was also not impressed when using the bathroom.

'Auntie... there is no toilet paper,' he yelled downstairs.

'Yes, there is,' said his great-aunt. 'It's pink.'

'That's not toilet paper. It hasn't got writing on it,' was his indignant reply.

The church in South Woodford had sent us the *Guardian Weekly* by airmail. When we finished reading it, I carefully cut it up into neat squares, strung the sheets together, and put them in our toilet without any great explanation to Mark that this was no longer normal in Britain. Occasionally, we were blessed with proper toilet paper. Geoff's parents and my stepmother always wrapped our Christmas presents in the stuff. It was eagerly retrieved before Mark and Rachel did it any damage!

Finding birthday and Christmas presents for the children was a problem. They had very few toys to play with in India. The local shops had little that they liked. We needed to be inventive. One year I got a carpenter to make a box with compartments for Mark. Then I asked our parents to send out Dinky cars. Another time we hauled a tricycle off a dump, repaired and repainted it. There was a Christmas when no mail arrived. I was getting desperate to buy something for Rachel. I wandered up and down the bazaar. Nothing. Until I spotted a family planning centre. (The government was trying to persuade families to have less children.) In the window was a set of dolls that fitted inside one another, rather like Russian wooden dolls – Mum, Dad and two children. There was Rachel's present. I rushed in and persuaded the staff to part with their window display.

*****

148

What followed next was one of the toughest years of my adult life. These days you would call it 'a perfect storm', except that it was considerably less than perfect as far as I was concerned. Perhaps I could have ridden one or two of the problems Geoff and I faced on our return. After all, I had more than negotiated the ripples and rollers of life in India. But now I was about to be swamped by circumstances and left floundering.

Once Geoff had returned and his mother was coping better, we moved into new accommodation; an attic flat in a three-storey, narrow terrace house just off the main shopping street in Minehead. There was one bedroom for the four of us and a tiny kitchen. I bought a little oven with a hot plate on top to do all my cooking. The bathroom with no loo was on the landing and the toilet one floor down. There wasn't a washing machine of any description. I needed to lug our clothes to and from the launderette two or three times a week. In many ways I was back to the same stresses of life in North London when Geoff and I were first married, except we now had two children. It goes without saying that this was never going to work for us as a family, but there was no other option.

Helping the children adjust, settling Mark into our old primary school, and maintaining the household was almost entirely down to me. RBMU had set up a year's deputation for Geoff – visiting churches to talk about our work in India and raise finances for our return. Unfortunately, the planning was haphazard to say the least. He would scoot up to Scotland for a week, taking our car, and then disappear down to Devon the next. We also struggled financially. RBMU's allowance, always fragile, just didn't meet our needs.

What finally pushed me over the edge was the future. RBMU had lined up a job for Geoff at a Bible seminary in Allahabad, Uttar Pradesh, half a day west of Muzaffarpur. He was going to be a tutor in 'Theological Education by

Extension'. Geoff was really excited about it. This was a new scheme; providing teaching for students where they were living and working, rather than bringing them into college fulltime. He would also be preparing materials up to degree level. What is more, there was a leprosy hospital over the river where I could work. It sounded 'perfect' for us.

The trouble was the children's schooling. There was nowhere in Allahabad for them to go. RBMU's remedy was to send them to a Christian international school in south India, a thousand miles away. We would see them for a month in the summer, when we could visit them, and for a month at Christmas, when they came home.

I just couldn't do it. With my childhood, there was no way I would let them go. My experiences at eight and nine years old cast very long shadows. I offered to go with the children and leave Geoff at the seminary, but our discussions with the mission stumbled. They wouldn't agree to Geoff and I being separated. It became clear we would have to leave RBMU. I felt guilty. This was my fault. And so, I fell, and fell hard into clinical depression.

Geoff was hit for six. His vision for the future shattered. It was clear that I was not going to return to India any time soon. Suddenly, instead of packing our bags, he had an ill wife and two small children on his hands, while he tried to maintain the mission's speaking schedule. His only alternative was to get a job in the UK as a pastor, something he had little desire to do.

We were very fortunate to be put in contact with a well-known, Christian psychiatrist, one Montagu Barker, who was based in Bristol. He was Scottish and forthright. He quite tore into Geoff, when Geoff explained his dilemma about wanting to be overseas and not wanting to be an 'ordinary' pastor.

'Your family is more important than your work,' he declared emphatically.

Not a pleasant episode for my husband to endure, but he graciously accepted that his vision must be ditched. He had to trust God to sort out the situation.

It took me eighteen months of medication to get over my illness. In the autumn we were able to find a holiday cottage to rent, a move which helped considerably. Hard as it was to leave the mission, RBMU later invited Geoff on to the UK board, a position which opened the door to him rejoining the mission four years later. Then Geoff's uncle contacted us. He was the minister at a church in Brixham, Devon. A small church in Torquay was looking for a pastor. Was Geoff interested? Calm to my perfect storm it turned out was at the far end of the A380.

*****

Hele (pronounced 'heel') Road Baptist was *The Little Church with the Big Welcome* – according to the noticeboard. Everyone knew it. When buses pulled up at the stop outside the church, drivers used to shout 'Little church with the big welcome!', so passengers were in no doubt about who we were. Conversely, there were the expected jokes about us being 'down at heel' and 'Hell Road', but actually it was a lovely church.

When we arrived Geoff would get sixty to seventy in the congregation. Most of our families came from the council estates around the church. After a few weeks one of the young people asked me:

'Please... Can you ask your husband not to use such long words? We don't understand him.'

That little conundrum sorted, what was amazing was the response to the preaching and teaching. In Muzaffarpur we had only seen one person baptised in five years. At Hele lots of folk made a decision to follow Jesus. By the time we left, four years later, there were over a hundred squeezing into the church on Sunday morning. God blessed us in a way we could never have expected as I struggled with depression and Geoff with his unfulfilled desires to return to India.

A lot of other things fell into place for us. The children had adapted well to being British. They had quickly discarded their 'Indian-ness', so they could be like their friends. They knew that squatting on their haunches, feet flat to the ground, while waiting for me in shops was likely to invite comment. Their 'Muzaffarpur' accents, which other children laughed at, were gone. At their request we had stopped using Hindi at mealtimes. Now they were in good schools. Rachel was doing well. Like me, Mark was dyslexic and a bit behind in his class. At Hele he got help with his reading from a headmistress who came to the church. He also excelled at art, which gave him confidence.

The church had a manse, but this had been bought for a single man, not a family. The leaders, however, agreed to build an extension. I got a new kitchen and Geoff moved his bedroom office into the old one. I successfully applied for a job at Torbay Hospital. I worked one night a week, ten to twelve hours, in the gynaecology department. I really enjoyed being a nurse again. Plus, it helped with our finances. Life was more comfortable than it had been in a long while.

Looking back, those four years were not just a happy time but a time of healing. God knew his plans for us, even if we didn't. Despite his doubts, Hele proved a great place for Geoff. The rapid growth of the church under his ministry was something to be grateful for. Mark and Rachel were settled. I was able to put the stresses I had suffered behind me. So, when RBMU asked Geoff to become director of the mission in the UK, it was a wrench to leave Torquay. We would be swapping the seaside for south London and, strangely, a small church with a big congregation for a much bigger church with a smaller one.

There was, however, one tragedy while we were at Hele that interrupted our happiness. In August 1974 I got a message from my stepmother. My father was missing at sea, presumed dead.

Chapter 21

Over Seas

Following his trips to Australia, my Dad had become a steward on transatlantic voyages, eventually working in the library on the QE2, Cunard's poster ship. That must have been quite a job – the library had around six thousand books and eighteen hundred passengers to keep tabs on. I have a couple of photos of him looking very dapper in a bright yellow jacket, white shirt and black bowtie. He also had his army ribbon firmly on display above his steward's badge. Perhaps it gave him something to chat to the passengers about. His badge gives his name as 'Bob', a nickname he liked to use although I have no idea why.

I have no idea what happened to him. All I know is what the official report told us and that wasn't much. The QE2 had docked at New York and was on its return voyage to Southampton. It seems my father got on the ship but then went missing. His colleagues, like good mates, covered for him, though they would have been better reporting his disappearance. The vessel was stopped mid-Atlantic. Needless to say, it was far too late to do anything useful.

Geoff and I left the children with Jean and her son, who were visiting Torquay, and went to Southampton. The captain was very kind and showed us around the ship, but there were few answers to our questions. Was it just an accident? A tragic loss of balance? Had he been up on deck for a smoke? I don't think he would have been drinking. A few weeks before, he and Stevie had visited us in Torquay. There was nothing to suggest he was depressed or ill. But how would I have really known? We were never as close as a daughter may hope.

In a strange way I had lost my mother to the mysteries of her mind. Now my Dad had left me in mysterious circumstances, but this time there was no note in my coat pocket to try and help me understand. The death certificate, when it was finally issued, simply stated 'Lost at Sea'. My stepmother didn't want a funeral or any kind of memorial, so my father slipped into our memories as quietly as he had apparently done beneath the waves of the Atlantic.

*****

I wasn't happy to be moving to London. I was pleased for Geoff though. The RBMU job was exactly what he wanted. The downside was that I got to see considerably less of him. Work was nine to five at the offices in Balham, away at meetings at the weekends, and trips abroad for six weeks a year. Still, with Mark and Rachel becoming more independent, I found another medical post – first as a nurse on the bank at St George's Hospital and then working in family planning clinics in Streatham and Tooting.

We did well with our next house, a semi-detached just down the road from Tooting Bec Common. It was owned by the mission and later we were able to buy it from them. We also acquired a new family member. Mark was desperate for a dog and, like many parents, we were finding it difficult to say no. Then one week Geoff was up in Manchester for a farewell for missionaries going overseas. They had a border collie, called Ben. Would we take him?

Geoff and I spent three evenings on the phone before I reluctantly agreed. Of course, this meant Geoff had to get Ben on the train up from Manchester to London and down the Northern Line to Clapham South tube station, as he had to visit the mission headquarters nearby before coming home. He did well until he was coming up the escalator at Clapham South. He had the dog, a dog basket, a bag of dog food, his briefcase, and his suitcase. Halfway up he lost his briefcase and watched it tumble all the way back to the bottom. So, he had to descend with the dog, dog basket, bag of dog food, and his suitcase, and then try again. It was a wonder we got him, the dog, and all their baggage into our car.

Our new church proved something of a mixed blessing. When we arrived, there were both Boys' and Girls' Brigades – Christian youth groups with plenty of activities on offer alongside Bible teaching. Mark and Rachel really enjoyed these. Sadly, the church went through several bad patches. Our first minister had an affair and had to leave. His replacement short-sightedly saw little value in the youth work and closed the brigades. As a result, we lost around a hundred children overnight; Mark and Rachel among them.

A few years later, Rachel went off to Europe on a Christian holiday with a group of young people. When she came home, she said:

'Mum, have you been praying for me?'

I thought, 'Oh, Lord, what do I say?' She had been very anti-church and I didn't want to say anything to upset her.

'You know I always pray for you…' I replied as tactfully as I could.

'Well, God spoke to me on the holiday and I've come back to him.'

I was delighted, of course. Geoff, unfortunately, was in the middle of the Congo, so he had to wait for that news.

A similar holiday, four years after this, also turned out to be a significant one for Rachel. She found herself a husband. On the coach on the way back one of the boys asked if he could see her again. She was a bit surprised. She didn't remember talking to him. Nevertheless, she agreed. It turned out to be a good reply.

Although Geoff was away from home a great deal, one of the pluses was that I was permitted to go with him on his overseas trips once in a while. I travelled to the Congo, Indonesia, Nepal and Peru. We also returned to India but didn't visit Muzaffarpur.

Nepal was wonderful. The churches in Kathmandu were amazing. Hundreds of Christians sitting on the floor, men on one side, women on the other, and the children running in between. The Congo left deep impressions. Again, the churches were vibrant. However, there were significant social problems to be addressed. Thankfully, child deaths had decreased, but the poor women were still bearing many children. They wanted me to talk to their husbands about using contraception. The men were not interested. They told me that having more children would make them richer.

When Mark was eighteen, we went to Peru and he came with us. Rachel preferred to stay in Streatham by herself. We visited a number of churches and went to a RBMU conference. We were also able to travel to Machu Picchu with a group of eight young people. We picked a great day to do this. The tourist train had broken down and we were the only ones there.

Indonesia was perhaps the most memorable trip. We went to Irian Jaya (now Papua). Our plane into the capital, Jakarta, was delayed and there was no-one to meet us, so we made our own way to the guest house. The cook firmly told us that the meal was finished, so if we wanted to eat, we would have to find it ourselves. Geoff and I wandered down to a local restaurant and looked at the menu. Not a word of English in sight, Geoff pointed at something and we hoped for the best. It turned out to be rice and a plate of pig's fat. I refused to eat it. Geoff somehow got it down.

From Jakarta we headed out to Irian Jaya and then off into the interior in a single engine plane belonging to Mission Aviation Fellowship. Our Dutch missionaries were there to meet us.

'Smile,' they told us. 'The people have put on their Sunday best.'

Of course, when we stepped off the plane, the whole welcoming party were naked. The women had a little grass skirt and the men wore gourds over their private parts. They were not in the least embarrassed. I didn't know where to look!

These tribal people were as remote as we were likely to find. The community lived mainly on sweet potatoes. Meat was limited to killing a pig once in a while. There was no money system. Everything was paid for in axes and pots and the like. The village women did most, if not all, of the work. They carried their babies in nets on their backs, while tending the gardens and cooking in their grass huts. Our Dutch colleagues were teaching them to grow fruit trees and vegetables to get a better diet, as well as helping them manage their pigs and raise a few chickens.

What was remarkable was that these people were all Christians, having been animists only a few years before. One Sunday, we were flown a ten-minute ride by helicopter to another mountain region to witness twenty baptisms. It would have taken us three days to walk there on foot; trekking down slippery paths, across treacherous fast flowing rivers, and up steep trails. The church members had dammed up a stream to create a pool. The water was so cold that the pastors could only baptise a couple of people before needing to get out and let someone else take over.

Afterwards, we had this astonishing pig feast. The village had dug a huge pit and filled it with stones, heated to red hot. Earth was layered onto the stones and then banana leaves, followed by strips of pork, more banana leaves, vegetables and more hot stones. Finally, earth was piled over the whole structure and the 'oven' left for twenty-four hours. When we sat down to eat, we were given little packets of salt as flavouring. The vegetables and meat were passed hand to hand. You took a bite of whatever you wanted and then passed it on. That was quite some BBQ.

The final joy was a communion service. The bread was sweet potato and the wine wild raspberry juice. Sitting out on the hillside, I found it quite emotional. Here I was in the depths of the Indonesian jungle, surrounded by hundreds of indigenous people. Irrespective of our histories, we were sharing a moment that goes back two thousand years – to the night Jesus and his disciples broke bread and took wine together; the night before he died on the cross.

When we left Irian Jaya, one of the villages presented us with a gift. A bow and a collection of arrows. The arrows were not all the same. When we asked why some were different, we were told that these were not used for killing animals. They were for humans. We hesitated to mention that as we carried them through customs...

Chapter 22

Another Adventure: Yangtze Calling

Did you know that I can drive a hovercraft? Not very well, it must be said. But, if I wanted to go to China with the British Hovercraft Expedition, this was one of the requirements. Every member of the team had to be familiar enough with the controls to point the craft roughly in the right direction and make it move.

I also learned new vocabulary. You can 'drive' a hovercraft. The craft have 'skirts'. 'Dump' and 'hump' are very important. 'Dump!' is something to shout (often in unison) before something on the hovercraft explodes. You can be over or below 'hump' – the wave that the hovercraft creates just ahead of itself. Being below hump is a bit like grinding along in first gear, when you would prefer to be in fifth.

You may drive a hovercraft, but it doesn't behave like a car I can tell you. Judging 'corners' is a little more fun. The craft drifts around bends. Going downstream is a wildly different experience to forging your way upstream. With the current behind you, the hovercraft can be riding the waves at fifty miles an hour. Another word of advice: it is never wise to use rocks as brakes.

In the autumn of 1989, a group of about thirty of us gathered on the banks of Lake Windermere, about a quarter of the way up on the left-hand side. The staff of the YMCA National Centre had been asked to devise a weekend activity programme for us. Our instructor, recently returned from an expedition to Everest, winkled us way out of our comfort zones. When we left, we were given a three-month exercise programme. Our medical team wanted us in 'peak fitness' before we left for Hong Kong in February. They were wise. We were going to be tested to our limits – trekking up to sixteen thousand feet in temperatures ranging from minus ten to thirty plus, heaving equipment in and out of vehicles, digging jeeps out of snow drifts, pushing lorries out of holes, pulling beleaguered hovercraft onto beaches.

We were a fascinating group. There was a good number of folk from the armed forces, bringing particular skills, alongside engineers, film crew, medics, scientists, a vet and a curate. Age-wise, we were by no means all young things. Our leader was in his fifties. I was forty-eight. And we had an artist with us, who was twenty years older than me.

Most of us were Christians, but there were a few who were not. One of them, a scientist, was amazed at how well we worked together in China.

'When my company has a project, they can take two years forming a team. And then it all falls apart because people just don't get on,' he told us. 'You hardly know each other. You're under amazing stress. But, if something goes wrong, no-one gets blamed. You all rally around to put it right.'

I think this team unity was a significant factor in him becoming a Christian.

Our objective – the one that caught the public imagination – was to take two hovercraft up the Yangtze River to its source. It goes without saying that this had not been done before. In fact, up to the 1970s the Chinese had apparently shown little interest in where Asia's longest river started. We would be the seventh expedition and the first to navigate our way upstream on the river itself. The source was high up on the Tibetan Plateau, but it was complicated. The official location was Jianggendiru, the Glacier of the Wolves, a forbidding place if ever there was one; a challenging landscape of biting cold, rarefied air and sharp ridges of ice. However, another expedition had wondered about an alternative location – a distant two hundred miles away. We had a sneaking ambition to visit both, though that proved impossible.

However, this expedition was not just about being the first to do something. Our boss, Squadron Leader Mike Cole, was adamant that there should be 'adventure with a purpose'. He had a heart to aid the poor. There would be a medical team led on the river by Dr Rachel (Ray) Pinniger. In addition, a lecturer from Loughborough University, Dr Mel Richardson, would test materials at altitude and in the difficult weather conditions we would endure. It seemed like a great package to offer the Chinese authorities. Unfortunately, our hosts didn't always show the same enthusiasm for the project that we did.

When I heard about the expedition, I was keen to enrol. China was a great mystery. I had been born on its borders but knew so little about it. What with Mao and his Bamboo Curtain, few westerners had been allowed there over the last forty years. Throughout the eighties, following Mao's death, the country had been gradually opening up. TV clips of blue-jacketed workers cycling to factories in their hundreds and dark-skinned (so-called) peasants in their pyramid hats ploughing rice paddies with oxen were an intriguing mix. The opportunity to see it for myself could not be missed. Plus, I could also go to Hong Kong, see where I was born, and visit the camp at Stanley.

I knew Mike Cole because he had run hovercraft expeditions to Nepal and Peru, countries where RBMU were working. I wrote to him offering my services as a nurse. He replied that the team had enough medical staff. Would I join the logistics team? I felt I was good at organising things, so I said 'yes'. Once there, I had a policy of getting stuck in where I was needed. In the end, I did far more nursing than logistics, but that was no problem as far as I was concerned.

What was difficult was the finance. Each team member had to raise five thousand pounds. We also had to agree to buy copies of the post-project book, written by one of the hovercraft drivers. This turned out to be a hefty hardback costing £12.95. I forget how many we had to purchase – a hundred perhaps – no small outlay on our return. I did a lot of speaking at church meetings to sell them all. Inevitably, Geoff and I had to make some sacrifices. However, I was working, so that helped. Money also came in from other sources. I was particularly grateful to a Swiss friend. He was a missionary but sent me a gift of a thousand pounds.

Dick Bell's book, *To the Source of the Yangtze*, gives far more detail of the expedition than I can here. There were years of planning, the purchase of the two hovercraft – the petrol driven *ICI River Rover* and the larger diesel craft, *Neste Enterprise*, both named after sponsors – the involvement of Ted Heath, ex-Prime Minister, and John Major, future PM, and a host of negotiations with dozens of people who provided funds, donated equipment, and generally kept the project afloat. However, with the team, hovercraft and all our baggage ready to head upriver, it looked like the project was going belly up in Hong Kong Harbour.

*****

Our troubles started at the press conference Mike held in the Hong Kong Yacht Club one Friday afternoon at the beginning of March 1990, the start of three days of activities. A high profile ceremony was arranged at City Hall. *Neste Enterprise* would be launched and give rides to orphanage and deaf children, as well as friends and families of local donors. We would feature on five regional radio stations, three TV networks, and in the newspapers. Despite the rain, it was to be a cheerful success. Hong Kong would be enthused.

The problem was the Chinese telex in Mike's pocket, received at the Yacht Club as the briefing started. When translated, it read:

'The contract has not been approved. Don't call press conference...'

Mike had a big decision to make: suffer the embarrassment of cancelling the weekend when it had already started or upset our hosts in China. He didn't bale out. He sent a message back. On the Tuesday five of the team would fly to Chengdu, the city in Sichuan Province from which we would set out, for further talks. Then he cleverly arranged for the rest of us to travel into China in small groups with a lot less fanfare. Within a week or so all the team would be in the country, with masses of equipment, and with the hovercraft sitting in gigantic blue containers at Chengdu's railway yard. It would then, he felt, be a little more difficult for the authorities to send us home.

I flew into Hong Kong from Heathrow, skimming the roof tops to land at Kai Tak Airport. A few days later, my group boarded the express train to the city of Guangzhou, from where we would fly to Chengdu. We travelled in first class comfort, a luxury that seemed a distant memory once we were bedding down in grimy guest houses or curling up in tents on cold gritty riverbanks. The crowded streets of Kowloon quickly disappeared. We trundled over the countryside of the New Territories and crossed the narrow river that marks the boundary into China.

It did seem as though the Chinese had cultivated every last square inch of land. Fields of beans, cabbages and cauliflowers competed for space with rice paddies and orchards of lemons and oranges. We saw peasants, women and men, stuttering along dirt tracks between mud huts, burdened beneath stacks of firewood or carrying pails, like old-fashioned scales, in pairs. All very picturesque, until we came to the industrial centres. Here the rivers ran like sewers and the countryside had turned grey. Chimneys belched black smoke into polluted skies. Workers caked in smut sank their spades into mountains of coal dust and loaded lorries that spewed noxious blue fumes onto the streets. If we had any concerns over health, we could have stopped right there and found more than enough to do.

Chengdu was less prosperous than Guangzhou, which then was some way behind the bustling wealth of Hong Kong. Our bus driver into the city clearly knew his rights as one of the larger vehicles on the roughly tarmacked roads. Bicycles, pedestrians, what few cars there were, and any animal that strayed into his path were blasted with his horn and survival was their responsibility, not his. We were housed at West China University of Medical Science, a large campus of curly roofed dormitories and teaching blocks, with ornamental dragons and snakes perched along the ridge tiles. There was a clock tower, a lake and pleasant tree-lined paths. It proved a real retreat from our ventures into the clamour of the city streets for which we were thankful – particularly given what happened next or, to be precise, what didn't.

We should have been in Chengdu for a few days, unpacking the hovercraft, loading them onto vehicles, starting out for the village of Dege, where we would begin the medical programme in earnest, and to Dengke, where the craft would be launched onto the Yangtze. It didn't work out that way. We were in the city for six or seven weeks, while our leaders sat with their Chinese counterparts and haggled over the contracts that needed to be signed before we could move on.

So, how do twenty odd Brits occupy themselves for a month and a half in a foreign city? We came up with a variety of answers. Praying for the success of the negotiations was high on the list of things to do. Some of us prayed more than we had ever done in our lives. We went sightseeing in Chengdu, went shopping in Chengdu, took a lot of photos of Chengdu. A cat-scarer was invented (another story altogether). And then there was formation cycling – the participants, dressed in their red expedition sweatshirts, parading up, down and around, keeping the locals bemused.

It proved a good opportunity to befriend students. They enjoyed speaking English. Playing volleyball and football with them became popular pastimes. Some were interested to know about our faith and request a Bible. Others were keen to get hold of denim jeans!

As time wore on, we began to disperse. There were trips to see the pandas. People climbed Mount Emei, a site sacred to Buddhists, not too far from Chengdu; no mean ascent to ten thousand feet. A few went north to Xian to find the Terracotta Warriors, or south to Kunming, China's Eternal Spring City. I was content to stay around Chengdu. In London I had met a Chinese girl whose parents lived in the city. She had asked me to take presents to them. They kindly invited me for meals and took me sightseeing. They were both scientists and on one occasion we visited their lab. It was beautifully laid out, but I couldn't see anyone at work. When I asked about experiments, they told me that they weren't doing any.

Eventually, the medical team got permission to lecture at hospitals and colleges. I was more than happy to volunteer to get involved. I was able to give masses of talks on family planning. This was a hot topic because of China's one child policy. State-imposed sanctions were fierce for anyone having a second baby. Contraception came in the form of the pill, coils and condoms, but abortion was frequently used to curtail pregnancies. It was good to feel I could do something useful.

Meanwhile, the bureaucratic nightmare that was our negotiating team's task was unfolding – often unravelling. Our presentation in Hong Kong, blatantly disobeying the authorities' instructions, had not gone down well. The Chinese side had lost face, an embarrassment of considerable consequence for them and us. In the background lurked a tangle of organisations, treacherously obstructing each other for reasons that had nothing to do with us. And there was always the issue of money. If they could squeeze another thousand yuan out of us here, there and wherever, so much the better. That said, some Chinese were eager to help us, despite the pressures and possible consequences for themselves, to whom we were grateful. We even got the public backing of Li Peng, their Prime Minister.

Contracts were devised, rewritten, torn up and glued back together. Permission was granted, then denied. There were some bizarre tactics. A key official went AWOL and was found hiding in the gatehouse. Customs denied that our hovercraft existed, even though our blue containers were sitting in their railway yard watching the steam trains go by. Team members with limited leave had to return to their jobs without even seeing the Yangtze. Until finally... finally, the message came through. Contracts were signed. We could leave Chengdu and head for Dege and Dengke taking our hovercraft with us, blessed with a ribbon cutting ceremony, Communist Party officials in suits and ties, a drum bashing band of local children, and the first unhindered sunshine we had seen in the city.

Chapter 23

Further Up and Further In

On 27 April, our team gathered by the hovercraft containers around a white Land Cruiser and a dusty, blue, open-backed lorry. It was 7.30 a.m. Dr Ray, our vet and logistics team, with me in tow, were anxious to get out of Chengdu and on the road to Dege. As we settled into our seats, a young Chinese woman slipped in alongside us. She, our Chinese host explained, would be a valuable help to us. She spoke excellent English. Her services would also cost us another thousand yuan. Once again, none too subtly, we were being asked to find extra money for equipment, drivers, engineers, guides and helpers we didn't need. Delay was inevitable as our team leaders haggled her out of the vehicle, unwilling to let her stay put unless she paid for herself.

We got to another 'finally' and our Land Cruiser eased away from the crowds of curious Chinese onlookers and onto the highway. It was then that we discovered that no-one seemed sure of the routes we were to take. Our maps left something to be desired. Bridges over rivers were promised and sometimes they were there and often they weren't. If we were looking for adventure, the remoter regions of Sichuan and Qinghai Province we were heading to were definitely going to deliver on that.

No matter where our Land Cruiser went, there were always people. Men in blue Mao jackets were selling long green poles of sugarcane or mending black shoes on the street corners of shabby towns that seemed too demoralised to expand into the surrounding paddy fields. There were young guys, wearing exactly the same as their fathers, leaning over outdoor pool tables. Women selling cigarettes chatted to grannies carrying babies. Food stall owners sweated over hot woks while trying to entice customers into their shops. Street sweepers pushed dust from one side of the road to the other with brooms made of branches and then swept it back again. Out on the hills, where landslides threatened to sweep us and them away, lines of workers, male and female, shored up the road with stones.

Somewhere in our three-day journey, we crossed into what we named 'Old Tibet' – a region much larger than what is called Tibet today. Here the byways were occupied almost entirely by dark-skinned Tibetans, a very different people from the Han Chinese whom we had been working with. The men liked hats – stiff stetson-style or baggy Mao caps – while the women braided their black hair into long plaits, held neatly in place by cloth bands. Deep red cloaks, jumpers and shirts, with splashes of yellow – colours associated with their religion – added some gaiety to their sombre jackets, trousers and skirts. We were eager to take photos, but we needed to be patient. It took a while for them to overcome their shyness. Mind you, if we were fascinated by them, they were equally happy to stare at us – weird western foreigners who were rarely allowed up into their homelands. It was odd to think that I may be the first white woman some of them had ever seen.

Religion was clearly an integral part of Tibetan life. Old women kept prayer wheels – small cylinders, containing handwritten mantras, rotating on wooden handles – in continuous motion. Strings of multicoloured flags, fluttering petitions on the wind, decorated the countryside. In more remote areas there were 'tents', some several feet high, made up of grey and red strips of material, each bearing a prayer. We saw dozens of small shrines sitting next to houses and visited a large temple, where rows of monks in red gowns and golden headdresses chanted mantras from memory, amidst the chinking of bells and the overpowering aroma of incense.

Our route took us into the mountains, travelling on dirt tracks cut into steep slopes. In the worst places we looked out queasily over sheer drops into distant valleys, praying fervently that our driver would keep all four wheels on the road. Not far from our destination we faced a huge challenge. Chola Pass is at sixteen thousand feet and beautiful, but the 'highway' was one long snow drift from start to finish. Lorries slid precariously to the very edge of safety. We dug ourselves and others out of icy ruts. One of the team suffered horribly from altitude sickness; a life-threatening illness, especially when the only way down to gentler heights is over the mountain ahead.

Finally – that word again – we drove into Dege, a 'two street county capital, straddling an apology for a river', as one of our team described it. We set up residence in a fairly insalubrious hotel, with a communal wash place and toilets that hung over the riverbed. Dege was the only place we had official permission for our much-reduced medical programme. Beyond this, anything we did would have to be done when our Chinese guides – minders, if you like – were not looking!

We got a great deal done. Over three days we carried out vaccinations for about five hundred children: diphtheria, whooping cough, measles, polio, tetanus and tuberculosis. Dr Ray offered the hospital one of eight possible lectures on basic health and caring for children. They asked for the lot. A team member showed how the solar fridges we had brought with us worked. Our vet found yaks and explained how they could carry the fridges, syringes and vaccines into the mountain villages. Despite the difficulties, we left the town feeling that we had achieved much, but that we could have done far more if we had been allowed to.

From Dege we headed north to what was our 'Base Camp 1' at a village called Dengke. Strange to say, we were a week into May and I had not yet seen what was the headline for our expedition – the Yangtze. Late one afternoon, we dropped down into a deep valley and wound around yet another 'zag' to match the 'zig' we had just negotiated. Then, suddenly, there was the river; a narrow steel coil of water, springing out of snow-capped mountains, snaking back and forth between high hills, caught by the sun. It was beautiful, exciting and a bit scary all at the same time.

In our absence, the hovercraft had just about survived a tortuous journey over the mountains to Dengke with other members of the team; *River Rover* perched uncomfortably on the back of a truck, *Enterprise* on a low-loader pulled by a startlingly orange lorry. Somewhat battered and bruised, the craft were waiting in our camp by the Yangtze for their first trips on the river. The local mayor had given the team a good welcome and the whole town two days holiday. It was great to discover that everyone was eager to assist us. Dozens of people helped clear the beach of boulders so we could drive the hovercraft onto the water. It took them ten hours of hard labour. When it was all done, speeches were made and the mayor cut a ribbon. Then, in front of around a thousand Tibetans, none of whom had seen these strange craft that moved on land and water, *River Rover* was launched and our first little piece of Yangtze history was made.

*****

You will know the familiar phrase about cats being away and mice playing. It was a little like that in Dengke. We had no official permission to provide any medical help, but it was clear to see that there were many needs. Thankfully, our Chinese minders went to bed at 6 p.m. Once they were out of the way, the Tibetan policeman with us went onto the streets and told people we had medicine if they came to see us. We did dressings, penicillin injections, handed out spectacles, and performed a whole host of small services to help our unauthorised patients.

One evening, a couple arrived clutching a sheepskin rug. I met them as they came in and thought they were trying to sell us the rug. However, the man gently unfolded it and showed me the baby he was carrying. It was clear the child was dying. Acute pneumonia, our team doctors said. While a dozen of us prayed, the medics gave the baby medicine. It seemed too little, far too late. Over the next few minutes, the baby's heart stopped three times. When Dr Ray handed the child back to the father, she had every intention of telling them to prepare for a funeral. Yet, as he took the baby into his arms, he tenderly blew over his child. Suddenly, the baby began to breathe again. It was a miracle that we thanked God for as the couple disappeared back into the darkness.

There were few opportunities to share our Christian faith. We were closely watched by our Communist guides. Nevertheless, we were free to have our own worship services, as long as we did not invite any local people. One Sunday, we made a circle of canvas chairs on the beach. We sang *Amazing Grace* to a guitar someone had brought with them. We read the story of God's ladder appearing to Jacob. We took communion together. It was a precious time. Around us, Tibetans on their ponies watched us with some bemusement, while our film crew took footage. Remarkably, for atheistic China, national TV aired this service as part of the expedition film a few months later.

Meeting a Tibetan Christian would have been next to impossible. Unless, of course, they came to find us. One evening, in another town, we were being put up on the top floor of a department store. There was a knock on the door and I went to open it. A couple of Tibetan men were standing there. One had a piece of paper in his hand. I was surprised to see the message was in English:

'We are Christians. Please do not tell. Have you Bibles?'

We prayed with them and filled their bags with Tibetan/English Bibles.

This was by no means the only opportunity. Another time, a Tibetan man stuffed a note in Mike's pocket, saying he 'loved Jesus'. Later, he turned up at our hostel with his family. We played cat and mouse with our minders until we got a few free moments to enquire what he wanted. With the broken English he had learned from the radio and using a dictionary to write a note, he asked for a New Testament. We were more than happy to oblige.

*****

River Rover and *Enterprise* were sent out on the river from Dengke a number of times, with varying degrees of success. Erratic currents, large boulders and fearsome rapids created hazards and caused serious damage. According to one of the hovercraft drivers there are different types of rapids:

Delightful – made for 'bumbling' up and down on.

Intriguing – where you chose your path carefully and don't have problems.

Exciting – not dangerous, but a water fight of a different kind.

Adventurous – where with God on your side, you will make it.

Impossible – when you should walk, preferably in the other direction.

Most of my river trips were in the first three categories, but there was one I will not forget.

On one trip *Enterprise* had come a cropper on rapids, crunching a rock downstream. The craft needed major repairs to its skirt before it could go any further. Another group of us were in *River* Rover, some distance behind. If we hadn't seen two team members waving an alert on the river bank, we may well have run into the rocks ourselves.

River Rover needed to go back to Dengke for help. However, there were now too many people for our smaller craft, so we took turns to walk. Two of us took the first walking stint and then I got back in again at the pick-up point. No sooner had we started upriver than we hit rapids. Again, we shed passengers, while one of the engineers, Neil, and I remained on the craft and tried to get over the rapid ahead of us.

It was one of the most frightening times of my life. The wind had strengthened and was swirling around. The waves slapped hard at the skirt. Neil grappled with steering, trying to avoid rocks. The black river boiled beneath us, threatening to tip us over. The hovercraft kicked into the air and then was sucked down beneath the water. I began to believe we were not going to make it. We would by no means be the first to have died trying to navigate rapids on the Yangtze.

'You drive. I'll pray,' I shouted.

I prayed out loud. I can't say the wind fell and the waves calmed, but Neil drove us forward and somehow – with God on our side – we made it. I was badly shaken up, though I tried not to show it. At the next stop I got out and walked for a while.

Our engineers did an amazing job of keeping the two hovercraft going, but it was clear that any plan to drive them upstream to Base Camp 2 – a place called Qumalai, a hundred and seventy miles north and a lot further along a river strewn with obstacles – was too ambitious. The two craft would have to be loaded onto their lorries and taken by road. Our quest to reach the source needed to start further up and further in.

*****

My journey to the source of the Yangtze ended at Qumalai. This little town was at the distant end of a remote cul-de-sac, eight days from Dengke. For such an inaccessible region it was surprisingly well organised. The streets were laid out in a grid pattern and the houses hidden behind walled compounds. The climate was horrible. There were dust storms and snow, high winds and hail. At night, we suffered from frost and needed jumpers. By breakfast, we were sweltering at thirty degrees plus. We were now at over thirteen thousand feet. If we worked for more than a few minutes, we became breathless. Taking frequent breaks was the only way to get anything done.

Our first problem was that when we got to Qumalai, we couldn't find the river. The Yangtze, we discovered, was about four miles away from the town. We trundled the hovercraft down an old quarry track, swamped in sand, that ran around a hill, past an abattoir, through a narrow valley and out onto a beach. It was here we set up camp, our tents hugging the river edge. There was no fresh water immediately available. This had to be lugged from a stream a quarter of a mile away each day, until someone had the bright idea of floating barrels downstream.

The next few days were spent preparing the craft, taking test runs on the river. I helped to set up fuel dumps further upstream, ready for the final push to the source. Unfortunately, it was not possible for us all to see our adventure to its destination. Mike called us together at Qumalai and explained the situation. There were around twenty-two of us left. Some had run out of time and now must return home. People were needed to guard equipment and take care of the fuel dumps, while others travelled on. It was disappointing not to be able to board the hovercraft headed for the source, but we still had parts to play if the expedition was to meet its goal.

The following Sunday we gathered on the river bank for our service. It would be the last time we could worship together and commit our journeys ahead to God. We sat by the Yangtze on a beautiful blue-skied day and sang *God of Glory, We Exalt Your Name*. And then, three days later, I waved the craft and crew goodbye as they set off upriver for their final adventure.

*****

For over a week I and the others left behind busied ourselves as best we could with whatever tasks needed to be done and wondered what had happened to the hovercraft. Finally,

Enterprise came into view on the river and the crew were at last able to tell us their story. *River Rover* had been dumped upriver some miles from the source and was going home on the back of a lorry. However, the *Enterprise* team, now down to ten, had driven on. By Monday 11 June they had come to a point in the river close to the official source where thick slabs of ice severely narrowed the running water of the Yangtze to no more than a few yards wide in places. Ripping the skirt apart was a distinct likelihood if they tried to go any further. Hovering over pitted ice was not possible. Black clouds were gathering above the Glacier of the Wolves. The team sensibly agreed that they had gone as far as they possibly could. This was the navigable source for a hovercraft – an achievement recognised by the Guinness Book of Records. They stepped out onto the icy riverbank, waved the flags of Britain, China and Finland (for our sponsor), took a few photos, and turned the *Enterprise* around.

We had done it.

Chapter 24

Reflections in a Photo

I have a photo, taken by Geoff, of myself in a red sleeveless top and long patterned skirt perched on a wall in Hong Kong. The sky is a pale blue, the sun lost for a while behind veils of fine white cloud. Behind me there is a building covered in bamboo scaffolding. The building's name is clear – Matilda Hospital. I do not remember whether it was deliberate, but I am sitting in front of a sign, which reads 'Matilda Child' (a direction to the Child Development Centre). This is what I am. This is the hospital where I was born.

Once the *Enterprise* had returned to Qumalai, what was left of the expedition team dispersed, making our own way home. I travelled with a couple of others, by road and train, and then on an overnight boat into Hong Kong. We had to bribe the ticket man to give us three berths as we didn't have enough money on us. (Yes, I know, Christians!)

In Hong Kong I met up with Geoff. It was a jubilant reunion. We had been apart for three and a half months. I was both glad and slightly miffed to discover he, Mark and Rachel hadn't really missed my home keeping. They had got on with perfectly well with the shopping and cooking without me.

Over the next few days we climbed the hill to Matilda and travelled out to Stanley. I was sad not to be able to see the campsite itself. The area was dominated by the prison and the college. We had to content ourselves with walking around the cemetery, looking at the graves of people I had been interned with. Poignantly, we came across a wreath laid by ex-members of the Royal Army Medical Corps, my Dad's old unit. The attached calligraphy beautifully honoured those who had died in the defence of Hong Kong and as POWS. More amusing was a notice requesting people to respect the dead, by not playing games amongst the graves, nor cooking food. I can't say I know many people who like to BBQ in cemeteries.

In my photo I am gazing off into the distance. There is a chance that I am wondering why Geoff is taking so long to take the picture, but I like to think that the photo captures a moment of reflection about the past. I had come a long way since my mother gave birth to me, my father hurried off to consult his mates about my name, and I became the girl who lived in a drawer. My Mum was still in the home near Basingstoke and would be for another four years. My Dad had been gone sixteen years. Unbeknown to us, we were about to lose my stepmother as well, just a few months after our return.

Elsewhere in the family there was good reason to be content. Geoff's parents were doing well in Minehead, despite his mother's ongoing frailties. Both Mark, now an architect, and Rachel, an accounts clerk, were getting established. Within a couple of years, Rachel would be getting married to Geraint and, as it turned out, giving us three wonderful grandchildren, Aaron, Matthew and Amy. Nevertheless, as we enjoyed our reunion in Hong Kong, Geoff and I knew we were just a few months away from yet another upheaval in our lives.

*****

All was not well in the world of Regions Beyond Missionary Union. It had been in existence for over a hundred years. Now there were serious questions over whether it could continue. The British part of the organisation, of which Geoff was the director, had long since split with its North American and Australian partners over differences on how the mission was run and Christian cultural issues. All very friendly, but Britain had been left to work on alone. The problem was that RBMU was running a late twentieth century mission using a century old structure. Admin costs were swallowing money that could have been used overseas. Its missionaries were dotted in countries all across the globe; very diverse situations, very far apart. A year after my China trip, RBMU in the UK was to close for good. Its remaining workers joined other organisations. Significantly, our friends in Peru became part of a new mission, Latin Link, which drew on the enthusiasm, expertise and advice of South American Christians. What the Grattan Guinnesses had started, my husband was going to have to bring to an end.

It was no easy job for Geoff to talk to each of the missionaries. Reactions were mixed. Some wanted to fight the decision. Others were shattered. They had all sacrificed a huge amount in joining RBMU – careers, finances, for some the possibility of marriage and family life. Needless to say, although he was pleased that all the RBMU personnel were able to continue their work with other agencies, this took a great deal emotionally out of Geoff. When the office doors were locked for the last time, he needed time before taking on another role. He chose to do a Diploma in Pastoral Studies in Bristol. We were fortunate that the house was no longer tied to his job. While there were pressures on our mortgage, at least we did not need to move until we were ready.

A year later Geoff was back in ministry. As usual, I was not happy as I might have been. I hated the thought of all the work involved, but it was what he felt God was calling him to. He became Associate Pastor (and later Senior Pastor) at a Baptist church in Godmanchester, north-west of Cambridge. We sold our house in London, Geoff's parents sold theirs in Minehead, and we found a new five-bedroom home together, just ten minutes' walk from the church. Having said that, you could walk from one end of the town to the other in less than twice that. Daily life was suddenly very different from living in London.

To be frank, the new house was a bombsite. In the recession of the early Nineties the owner had lost it due to bank repossession. Angry, she had broken things and pettily removed door catches, cut the washing line, and taken the front door knocker with her. Still, once we had put it to rights and repainted, it served us well for eighteen years. We were blessed that Mark also moved in with us until he bought his own home in the town. He was looking for a new job after finishing his postgraduate degree. As a qualified architect he proved very handy with a paintbrush!

Having Geoff's parents with us also worked well. Mark put his training to work, redesigning the house to provide a granny flat and lovely garden for them. They had their own entrance and we converted the cupboard under the stairs into a kitchen, while we mainly lived upstairs. By this stage Geoff's Mum was a semi-invalid. His father had cared for her for many years and had done an excellent job. One day in June 1998 he called me in because he was worried. My mother-in-law was lying on the sofa. Suddenly, her face fell, her arm went. She was having another stroke. Within thirty seconds she was gone. It was a not a surprise, but it was a great sadness.

Geoff's Dad found something of a new lease of life once the worry of caring for his wife had gone. He preached. He went to every church event he could. Somehow, he got himself invited to the women's meetings, the only man there. He also put the artistic talents which he passed on to Mark to good use. Amongst the many watercolours he did, he painted a picture of the local surgery, which still hangs on a wall there. Whenever he went to the doctors for treatment, he made it an opportunity to invite the nurses around to 'his flat' for supper. There was no doubt that he thoroughly enjoyed his final years!

As far as the church was concerned, I tried to keep a low profile. Hospitality was my best gift. We often invited around ten people for lunch on a Sunday. Geoff's Dad kept them entertained in his part of the house until I was ready.

When he finally passed away, we opened up his rooms as a bed and breakfast for relatives of patients at the famous heart hospital down the road at Papworth.

As well as the death of Geoff's Mum, there were other shadows that crossed our paths. Swamped by stress I suffered two further bouts of clinical depression. In both cases it took the best part of a year to get over it. The medication seemed less effective than when I had taken it on the previous occasion in Minehead. The second episode was particularly bad. It came as a result of a terrible accident that Mark was involved in. One evening, he was out on his motorbike and came off very badly in a collision. Around midnight, we were called to Bedford Hospital. When we arrived, the doctors didn't want me to see him. I told them I was a nurse, I was his mother, and I needed to. He was in a terrible state. I had to walk through his blood on the floor to get to the bed.

The right side of his body was shattered. He had broken about twenty-five bones. They gave him forty bags of blood to keep him alive. The hospital clearly did not have the facilities to deal with his injuries. Should he be airlifted to London or use an ambulance to get him to Cambridge? We opted for Cambridge because Addenbrookes Hospital had a surgeon on call who could operate straight away on Mark's internal injuries.

There were four medics in the vehicle and we followed on behind.

'If we stop and turn around,' they told us, 'you will know he has died. Cambridge won't accept a dead body.'

It was a long journey, but he made it and so did we. It took nearly a year to get him back on his feet. As a result, he lost his job and eventually headed up to Newcastle to start again. The downside from my point of view was the depression. As soon as Mark was better, I went into steep decline. It was my turn to be in hospital – for a month.

*****

As I sat outside Matilda Hospital in Hong Kong in 1990, all this was ahead of me. I could reflect on the past and only wonder about the future. Amidst the memories of my parents and Stanley, there was perhaps another thought that briefly pushed its way to the forefront and then was hurried back to its place, buried as deeply as I could manage. Nevertheless, it was a problem I was going to have to address. It was not so much an elephant in the room of my life, more a whole nation of people; one hundred and twenty-three million of them.

Chapter 25

When God Smiled

Going to church can get troublesome.

On the Sunday morning that Geoff started as Associate Pastor at Godmanchester Baptist I doubt I was giving Japan much thought. It was a big day for Geoff and I needed to be alongside him as the new minister's wife. I would be meeting people whose names I must remember, discovering who was related to whom, finding out who did what, and beginning to discover where I would fit in.

I wonder if God was smiling to himself as I walked cheerfully across the tarmacked car park and through the double doors. Sitting in the church seats was an Asian family. And across the way another one. Very welcome, of course. Except that both these families were Japanese. I was severely shaken out of my sense of well-being.

'I don't think I can cope,' I cried at Geoff later.

He was not at all sympathetic. 'Well, you'll just have to get on with it,' he said.

I know a lot of people hated the Japanese after the war. Soldiers and civilians who had suffered in the camps, relatives who knew what had happened to husbands and sons, wives and daughters. As the stories of atrocities began to emerge, few Brits had a good word for the 'Japs'. I wasn't like that, I thought. Yet, as I walked into the church, I realised that I blamed them for all that had happened to my family. My dislike of all things Japanese – I wouldn't buy anything made in Japan – was subconscious, but it was as real as the problem I now faced.

'I can't be here... with these people,' I said to myself as I took my seat.

Nevertheless, Geoff was right, bless him. I was going to have to face up to myself.

This was no easy task. I didn't want to be in Godmanchester. I certainly didn't want to be at the church. I was going to need God's help to sort this one out. I prayed. A lot. And then a lot more.

What made the difference were the families themselves. They were just so friendly; genuinely nice people, so unlike my image of their nation. Moreover, they were Christians. I had met, prayed and worshipped with Congolese Christians, Indian Christians, Nepalese Christians, Peruvian Christians, Chinese and Tibetan Christians, and a heavenly host of other nationalities. How could I exclude these good folk sitting in the seats next to me? It took me a while, but slowly I came to love them. One couple in particular, Kiku and Tamiko Horinouchi, with their four children, became great friends.

It would have been nice to leave it there, but this was only a first step. Kiku and Tamiko had listened to my stories of Stanley Camp and what happened to my mother and father. They were keen for me to meet a Japanese woman who was coming to Cambridge to speak at churches. She was talking about reconciliation. I recoiled at the idea. Having Japanese friends was one thing, forgiving the nation was another.

Keiko Holmes was slight, immaculately dressed in a kimono, and surprisingly direct. She had started an organisation, Agape World. Her aim was to help POWs and internees to find healing from the hatred that haunted their lives.

Her own story was very powerful. She had grown up in the secluded forested hills of Mie Prefecture, about sixty miles south of Osaka, where my Dad had been imprisoned. After high school she had moved to Tokyo to study English. There she had met and married a Christian British businessman, Paul Holmes, who had originally come to Japan on a six-month contract. Tragically, eighteen years later, Paul's death in a plane accident while overseas had left her in a dark place. While visiting her home in Japan some years afterwards, she had revisited a memorial to sixteen British soldiers in a neighbouring village called Iruka. She was amazed to discover that the rather simple site with its rough stones, tired white wooden cross, and meagre picket fence had been transformed. Now there was a small but well-kept commemorative garden decorated with expensive orchids, a large copper cross, and the names of the men engraved in marble. These were POWs who had worked in a mine nearby. What was moving was that, years after the war ended, the grave was being neatly maintained by locals.

Keiko returned to the UK with fresh, God-given purpose in her life. She was determined to find the relatives of these men and tell them about the memorial. Somehow, she would arrange for them to travel to Iruka and see it for themselves. What she met was a wall of rejection. Few POWs had time for her. The hatred of her and her nation was palpable.

Astonishingly, given the aggressive opposition, Keiko had persevered. A tour to Japan was organised the year we arrived in Godmanchester. A decade later she had been honoured with an OBE and in 2018 received the *Order of the Rising Sun: Gold and Silver Rays* from the Japanese Emperor, both awards for her reconciliation work.

That tour in 1992 was the first of many. From them came dozens of testimonies of how reluctant travellers, POWs and internees like myself, had found healing through these trips to Japan.

In 2004, Keiko asked us, 'Would you like to go on the Pilgrimage of Reconciliation this year?'

I said yes.

*****

Flying into Tokyo that October was an odd experience. For someone who had avoided the Japanese for decades, I was about to find myself completely submerged by the people and their culture. Bowing technique, slipper etiquette, politeness personified. Strings of cities crammed into small spaces between the sea and the mountains. The famed bullet trains and four lane toll roads. Sushi, okonomiyaki, and miso soup. Hot springs and (single-sex) communal bathing – in the nude! How much submergence did I need?

There were around eighteen of us in the group. Tamiko, who had temporarily moved back to Japan, kindly travelled with us, acting as our translator. One or two of the older men had been on the Hell Ships into Japan. As we listened to their moving stories, I began to understand what my father had endured. We did visit Osaka, but at the time I didn't know that was where my Dad had been, so it held no particular significance for me.

To say we went everywhere would be an exaggeration, but it did feel like an on-the-road, don't-stop-here-too-long three weeks. We attended dozens of meetings. The ones in the universities and schools were particularly worthwhile. The students listened in silence to our stories. For many of them this was the first time they had really become aware of the events of the war. Their textbooks were as quiet on their army's treatment of POWs and internees as they were.

We travelled to Iruka and gathered in the memorial garden for a service. It is not a particularly scenic spot. Yet, there is something peaceful about the place that allows you to pull away for a few moments. We were deeply touched by the kindness of the local population, who, knowing that the British relatives would not be able to honour their dead, had kept the memorial so beautifully. They too had suffered in the war.

Hiroshima is one of those cities that you must visit if you go to Japan. It stands on a river delta, a flat open area. On 6 August 1945 a speck of a plane flew over the city as its citizens were getting ready for work. Unlike many bombs,

America's new atomic weapon, 'Little Boy', was not designed to be flung at its target. It floated down on a parachute and exploded in the air, doing the worst possible destruction.

Photos in the Hiroshima museum show a landscape almost bereft of buildings, stripped of life. There is a collection of melted bottles, roof tiles that look like lumps of lava, broken and twisted girders, shredded clothing, and the burnt remains of a tricycle and helmet belonging to a three-year-old. Displays narrate the fury of firestorms and tell the story of black radioactive rain. The grim horror of burnt and broken bodies is all too graphically evident in the pictures that line the walls. There is a stone with the shadow of a person imprinted on it. Our visit was sobering to say the least.

Yet, and here I had to pause, I knew that this bomb had saved my life. I had survived because others had died. Holding this suffering and my own together is almost impossible. Or it would be, if it wasn't for what also happened on that trip to Japan.

As a group we visited Kyoto, the famous old capital of Japan. Down the road is another, less well-known, bygone capital; a city called Otsu, which sits at the southern end of Japan's largest lake, Biwa. One Sunday morning, we attended the Baptist church there. We had no trouble locating it. A huge cross standing about thirty foot up above a modern vivid red-roofed building and large English lettering fronting the highway by the lake left us in no doubt that we had found the right place.

We were guided to the front of the church. Seated close by was a Japanese man in a suit, about my height, looking a little nervous. During the service he came to the lectern and was introduced to us. He had been a guard at one of the prison camps. (I seem to remember this was one of the many camps in Japan, though I don't recall which one.) Now, he said, he was a Christian.

The pastor was looking at us. At me.

'Would you be willing to come forward? Perhaps you would be able to greet each other.'

Slowly, I got up from my seat. The man was no more than a yard away across the red carpet, but it felt as though I needed to cross oceans to stand in front of him.

I have to say, it was with great reluctance that I lifted my hand and offered it to him.

His hand touched mine. Just briefly. The kind of polite shake you expect from a stranger.

And then a huge burden rolled from my shoulders. It was physical. It was spiritual. It was releasing. The anger and hurt over what had happened to my family and to me were gone – as though they had never been there at all. Miraculously, I felt a freedom I had never experienced since as far back as I could remember.

I sat down and looked beyond the pastor to the image of the cross on the wall. This is where we had met, this Japanese guard and I. This was where I had finally found healing. Beneath the cross of Christ. God, I felt, must be smiling.

Epilogue

That is just about my story. Except, like all good biographies, I need to bring you up to date on what happened to Geoff and me.

Two years after our trip to Japan, I went again. This time with Jean. We travelled to much the same places and did similar things. I hope that it proved as helpful to her as it did to me. That was also the year that Geoff's Dad died, aged ninety-three, and when Geoff retired as pastor of Godmanchester Baptist Church, having done an extra year so we could pay off our last mortgage.

We stayed on in Godmanchester for four years but moved denominations. We found an Anglican church on the other side of the A14 – St James, by the river at Hemingford Grey. All was going well until Geoff had a slight brain bleed. Now we needed to be nearer Rachel and her family. So, we sold up and moved south. We swapped a town mentioned in the Domesday Book with two Roman roads, for another with one – West Wickham, on the edge of Greater London.

We had no intention of retiring to the TV, much as we enjoy watching sport and travel programmes. Geoff preached and took services. He got involved with the Bible Society. Agape World asked him to become chairman of the board and I joined him as a trustee. He also served on the board of other charities. Anglo-Indian Concern was started by friends of ours in Godmanchester, aiding disadvantaged Anglo-Indians in Chennai. Starfish Asia, an organisation based near to our new home and whose founder we had met while in Muzaffarpur, mainly works with minority Christian children in Pakistan, providing help with their education.

It was through going to India with Anglo-Indian Concern that we were able to return to Muzaffarpur in 2007. Geoff found it quite emotional to be there, but I think I had said my goodbyes to India some time ago. We visited the churches and the Parsonage, as well as the leprosy hospital. The bookshop had gone and John Mathew had retired to Kerala in the south. After a long search we found our old home. It had been swallowed up in the expansion of the town. We couldn't believe just how small it was. How on earth had we lived there? Mind you, it was now being used as a school for a dozen children. We found one family in Muzaffarpur who remembered us and we had a meal with them. They were our former neighbours. The wife had been our language teacher back in 1966-1967!

In October 2018, we moved into a bungalow in a lovely sheltered housing complex in West Wickham. It was a good move for us. Earlier that year, Geoff had suffered a couple more brain bleeds, from which he thankfully made nearly a full recovery. Nevertheless, he hasn't entirely relinquished his ministry. Occasionally, he preaches and leads services in our local Anglican Church – St John's. As for myself, with a share in an allotment, I am still growing vegetables and fruit!

I guess as we approach our eighties we may have expected to settle down, but life has its little surprises. As I am writing this last part of my story, Mark and his partner, Ania, have given birth to Sofia Eva Larcombe, our precious fourth grandchild. And so, a new chapter of our lives has begun.

Acknowledgement

My thanks go to a lot of people who have helped in the writing of this book.

My husband, Geoff, has been a loving support during my life's journey. He has also been extremely helpful in filling in story details and especially good at remembering dates. I am also grateful to Mark and Rachel for reading the manuscript and making suggestions here and there to improve it. I am thrilled that Mark designed the book cover for me.

In the writing of the book, it was delightful to make contact with Robert – my 'lost' cousin – and Robyn Sterling. They provided great anecdotes, documents and photos from Leo's side of the family, which have unquestionably enhanced my own story.

I am thankful to Dr Ronald Clements for his research and in putting down my stories in words. Also to Bethan Ellish, who edited the manuscript. Revd. Dr Hugh Osgood, Keiko Holmes and Revd. Jon Ward were kind enough to read the book in advance of publication and provide endorsements. I have appreciated the help and advice given by the staff at New Generation Publishing, my publishers.

Clive and Dorothy Himsworth provided a lot of valuable reading material about the camps at Stanley and Shamshuipo. Tony Banham and David Bellis supplied fruitful contacts and their websites – www.hongkongwardiary.com and www.gwulo.com – were significant resources on Hong Kong and the internment camps. Information about the camp in Osaka came from www.mansell.com.

Closer to home, the Historical Disclosures Section of the British Army Personnel Centre sent me copies of my father's army records. Shirley Henderson of SASRA was able to give me information about Mr Hitchcock. Peter Gunner sent me a copy of the hovercraft expedition documentary. Others who provided timely help in various ways include Revd. Dr Anne Clements, Professor Mel Richardson and Tony Sharpe.

Writing this book enabled me engage again with the life of George Muller and the orphanage work he founded. The staff at Mullers – www.mullers.org – provided me with information about Hillbury and I was very happy to get copies of letters and the application forms that were completed when Jean and I went to Minehead. Being able to contact Margaret Carr after so many years was a wonderful surprise and I am grateful that she was able to write about her memories of me.

However, I want to finish with special mention of Phyllis Green – Mageen, my housemother. My deeply felt thanks go to her for the seven years she cared for me at Hillbury.

Authors' Notes

Chapter 2

'the comfort and recovery of the patients...'   Lord Palmerston, 1857, quoted in Lytton Strachey, *Eminent Victorians: Cardinal Manning, Florence Nightingale, Dr Arnold, General Gordon* (London: Chatto and Windus, 1918), p. 160.

'In the year 1878...'   Doyle, Arthur Conan. *A Study in Scarlet* (London: Ward Lock and Co, 1887), p. 13.

Chapter 3

'a riddle wrapped in a mystery...'   Winston Churchill, broadcast 1 October 1939, quoted by The Churchill Society, http://churchill-society-london.org.uk/RusnEnig.html (accessed 25 November 2019).

'A story went around...'   Reported in Steve Smith, *The Russian Revolution: A Short Introduction* (Oxford: Oxford University Press, 2002), p. 81.

'a wad of five hundred rouble notes...'   In the 1930s £1 was worth around 10 roubles.

Chapter 4

'the   trustees   of   [Granville   Sharp's]   estate...'
http://www.matilda.org/en/about/our-heritage (accessed 25 November 2019).

Chapter 5

'a barren island…' Lord Palmerston, 1841, quoted in Jean Gittins, *Stanley: Behind Barbed Wire* (Hong Kong: Hong Kong University Press, 1982), p. 3.

'Shamshuipo' Major Victor Ebbage gives a good account of life in Shamshuipo POW camp (*The Hard Way: Surviving Shamshuipo POW Camp 1941-45* [Brimscombe, Gloucestershire: Spellmount, The History Press, 2011]).

'a Chinese brothel…' Quoted on https://gwulo.com: attributed to Butterfield, R.P. *The Saturday Evening Post Treasury – Japanese Occupation of Hong Kong* (University of Michigan: Simon and Schuster, 1954), (accessed 25 November 2019).

Chapter 6

'Stanley' Two enlightening personal accounts of the time spent in Stanley camp are given by Jean Gittins (*Stanley: Behind Barbed Wire* [Hong Kong: Hong Kong University Press, 1982]) and John Stericker (*A Tear for the Dragon* [London: Arthur Barker Ltd, 1958]). Geoffrey Emerson provides a more academic account based on interviews with twenty-three internees (*Hong Kong Internment, 1942-1945: Life in the Japanese Civilian Camp at Stanley* [Hong Kong: Hong Kong University Press, 2008]).

Chapter 7

'Revd. Kiyoshi Watanabe' Revd. Kiyoshi Watanabe's story is told in Liam Nolan, *Small Man of Nanataki* (London: The Catholic Book Club, 1966).

Chapter 11

'For God so loved the world…'   John 3:16 (NIV).

Chapter 12

'wretched, pitiful, poor…'   Revelation 3:17 (NIV).

'Living he loved me…'   Chapman, J.W., *One Day When Heaven Was Filled With His Praises* (Public domain, 1910).

Chapter 16

'Henry Grattan Guinness'   Michele Guinness has written about the Guinness family history. Henry Grattan Guinness's story can be found in *The Guinness Spirit: Brewers and Bankers, Ministers and Missionaries* (London: Hodder and Stoughton, 1999).

'Regions Beyond Missionary Union'   The mission's name was taken from Paul's reference in his second letter to the Christians at Corinth that he wished to take the Christian message to the 'regions beyond' them (2 Corinthians 10:16 [NIV]). Years later, when he was CEO of RBMU in London, Geoff had a phone call from a man who wanted to know if RBMU was a trade union for overworked and underpaid missionaries. There was more than a grain of truth in his assumption!

'Kellogg Memorial Church'   The church was originally an American Presbyterian church and was re-named after Revd. Dr Samuel Kellogg, who ran the language school – not after a breakfast cereal. On Sundays, we occasionally went to Kellogg Memorial, but mainly attended the Anglican church. We were forbidden to go to the Pentecostal house church!

'forty-six letters' There are various opinions on how many letters there are, so you may see other totals given.

Chapter 18

'loving but exceedingly bracing' Elizabeth Pritchard, *Testimony of a Whatnot* (Lisburn: Ulster Friends Home Mission, 2008), p. 105.

Chapter 19

'it was not always a safe place…' The situation in the south of the country was quite different. Christians there trace the Church in India all the way back to Saint 'Doubting' Thomas, one of Jesus' first and closest disciples. According to tradition, after the death and resurrection of Jesus, Thomas travelled to India. He preached the good news about Jesus from the south-west coast to the east, before being murdered and buried in what is now Chennai.

'There goes Jehu' Jehu was one of the kings of Israel, who drove his chariot 'like a maniac'. 2 Kings 9:20 (NIV).

Chapter 22

'Yangtze Calling' Yangtze is the name we predominantly use for the river and so I have used it here. However, the river has various names along its length.

'*To the Source of the Yangtze*' Dick Bell, (London: Hodder and Stoughton, 1991).

Chapter 23

'Han Chinese' In my descriptions I have used 'Chinese' to refer to the people of China and of Hong Kong. The Han Chinese are the majority ethnic group in China.

'a village called Dengke' Following the Yangtze expedition, under the work of The Care and Share Foundation, Mel Richardson founded Project Dengke, providing ongoing help and aid to the region. http://www.projectdengke.com (accessed 25 November 2019).

'Amazing Grace' Newton, J., (Public domain, 1779).

'God of Glory...' Fellingham, D., *God of Glory, We Exalt Your Name* (Kingsway's Thankyou Music, 1982).

Lightning Source UK Ltd.
Milton Keynes UK
UKHW011927060320
359913UK00002B/167